SPEECH AND HEARING

GENERAL EDITORS

Dale C. Garell, M.D.
Medical Director, California Children Services, Department of Health
　Services, County of Los Angeles
Associate Dean for Curriculum; Clinical Professor, Department of Pediatrics &
　Family Medicine, University of Southern California School of Medicine
Former President, Society for Adolescent Medicine

Solomon H. Snyder, M.D.
Distinguished Service Professor of Neuroscience, Pharmacology, and
　Psychiatry, Johns Hopkins University School of Medicine
Former President, Society for Neuroscience
Albert Lasker Award in Medical Research, 1978

CONSULTING EDITORS

Robert W. Blum, M.D., Ph.D.
Associate Professor, School of Public Health and Department of
　Pediatrics
Director, Adolescent Health Program, University of Minnesota
Consultant, World Health Organization

Charles E. Irwin, Jr., M.D.
Associate Professor of Pediatrics; Director, Division of Adolescent
　Medicine, University of California, San Francisco

Lloyd J. Kolbe, Ph.D.
Chief, Office of School Health & Special Projects, Center for Health
　Promotion & Education, Centers for Disease Control
President, American School Health Association

Jordan J. Popkin
Director, Division of Federal Employee Occupational Health, U.S. Public
　Health Service Region I

Joseph L. Rauh, M.D.
Professor of Pediatrics and Medicine, Adolescent Medicine, Children's
　Hospital Medical Center, Cincinnati
Former President, Society for Adolescent Medicine

THE ENCYCLOPEDIA OF
HEALTH

THE HEALTHY BODY

Dale C. Garell, M.D. · General Editor

SPEECH AND HEARING

William D. Allstetter

Introduction by C. Everett Koop, M.D., Sc.D.
former Surgeon General, U. S. Public Health Service

CHELSEA HOUSE PUBLISHERS

New York · Philadelphia

The goal of the ENCYCLOPEDIA OF HEALTH *is to provide general information in the ever-changing areas of physiology, psychology, and related medical issues. The titles in this series are not intended to take the place of the professional advice of a physician or other health care professional.*

ON THE COVER False-color scanning electron micrograph of the surface of the organ of Corti, part of the cochlea of the inner ear. Hair cells, which appear as U-shaped lines at the top of the image, help convert mechanical movements caused by sound waves into electrical impulses that are transmitted to the brain through the auditory nerve.

Chelsea House Publishers
EDITOR-IN-CHIEF   Remmel Nunn
MANAGING EDITOR   Karyn Gullen Browne
COPY CHIEF   Juliann Barbato
PICTURE EDITOR   Adrian G. Allen
ART DIRECTOR   Maria Epes
DEPUTY COPY CHIEF   Mark Rifkin
ASSISTANT ART DIRECTOR   Noreen Romano
MANUFACTURING MANAGER   Gerald Levine
SYSTEMS MANAGER   Lindsey Ottman
PRODUCTION MANAGER   Joseph Romano
PRODUCTION COORDINATOR   Marie Claire Cebrián

The Encyclopedia of Health
SENIOR EDITOR   Brian Feinberg

Staff for SPEECH AND HEARING
COPY EDITOR   Joseph Roman
EDITORIAL ASSISTANT   Christopher Duffy
PICTURE RESEARCHER   Georganne Backman
DESIGNER   Robert Yaffe

First Printing
1 3 5 7 9 8 6 4 2

Library of Congress Cataloging-in-Publication Data

Allstetter, William D.
   I. Speech & hearing/by William D. Allstetter
      p.   cm.—(The Encyclopedia of health)
   Includes bibliographical references (p. 94).
   Summary: Examines the vital mechanisms of human communication, speech, and hearing through a discussion of the body's role in these functions.
   ISBN 0-7910-0029-X
        0-7910-0469-4 (pbk.)
   1. Speech—Juvenile literature. 2. Hearing—Juvenile literature. 3. Speech disorders—Juvenile literature. 4. Hearing disorders—Juvenile literature. [1. Speech 2. Hearing.] I. Title. II. Title: Speech and hearing. III. Series.   90-1718
QP399.A43 1991   CIP
612.7'8—dc20   AC

CONTENTS

THE ENCYCLOPEDIA OF
H E A L T H

THE HEALTHY BODY

The Circulatory System
Dental Health
The Digestive System
The Endocrine System
Exercise
Genetics & Heredity
The Human Body: An Overview
Hygiene
The Immune System
Memory & Learning
The Musculoskeletal System
The Nervous System
Nutrition
The Reproductive System
The Respiratory System
The Senses
Sleep
Speech & Hearing
Sports Medicine
Vision
Vitamins & Minerals

THE LIFE CYCLE

Adolescence
Adulthood
Aging
Childhood
Death & Dying
The Family
Friendship & Love
Pregnancy & Birth

MEDICAL ISSUES

Careers in Health Care
Environmental Health
Folk Medicine
Health Care Delivery
Holistic Medicine
Medical Ethics
Medical Fakes & Frauds
Medical Technology
Medicine & the Law
Occupational Health
Public Health

PSYCHOLOGICAL DISORDERS AND THEIR TREATMENT

Anxiety & Phobias
Child Abuse
Compulsive Behavior
Delinquency & Criminal Behavior
Depression
Diagnosing & Treating Mental Illness
Eating Habits & Disorders
Learning Disabilities
Mental Retardation
Personality Disorders
Schizophrenia
Stress Management
Suicide

MEDICAL DISORDERS AND THEIR TREATMENT

AIDS
Allergies
Alzheimer's Disease
Arthritis
Birth Defects
Cancer
The Common Cold
Diabetes
Emergency Medicine
Gynecological Disorders
Headaches
The Hospital
Kidney Disorders
Medical Diagnosis
The Mind-Body Connection
Mononucleosis and Other Infectious Diseases
Nuclear Medicine
Organ Transplants
Pain
Physical Handicaps
Poisons & Toxins
Prescription & OTC Drugs
Sexually Transmitted Diseases
Skin Disorders
Stroke & Heart Disease
Substance Abuse
Tropical Medicine

PREVENTION AND EDUCATION: THE KEYS TO GOOD HEALTH

C. Everett Koop, M.D., Sc.D.,
former Surgeon General,
U.S. Public Health Service

The issue of health education has received particular attention in recent years because of the presence of AIDS in the news. But our response to this particular tragedy points up a number of broader issues that doctors, public health officials, educators, and the public face. In particular, it points up the necessity for sound health education for citizens of all ages.

Over the past 25 years this country has been able to bring about dramatic declines in the death rates for heart disease, stroke, accidents, and for people under the age of 45, cancer. Today, Americans generally eat better and take better care of themselves than ever before. Thus, with the help of modern science and technology, they have a better chance of surviving serious—even catastrophic—illnesses. That's the good news.

But, like every phonograph record, there's a flip side, and one with special significance for young adults. According to a report issued in 1979 by Dr. Julius Richmond, my predecessor as Surgeon General, Americans aged 15 to 24 had a higher death rate in 1979 than they did 20 years earlier. The causes: violent death and injury, alcohol and drug abuse, unwanted pregnancies, and sexually transmitted diseases. Adolescents are particularly vulnerable because they are beginning to explore their own sexuality and perhaps to experiment with drugs. The need for educating young people is critical, and the price of neglect is high.

Yet even for the population as a whole, our health is still far from what it could be. Why? A 1974 Canadian government report attributed all death and disease to four broad elements: inadequacies in the health care system, behavioral factors or unhealthy life-styles, environmental hazards, and human biological factors.

To be sure, there are diseases that are still beyond the control of even our advanced medical knowledge and techniques. And despite yearnings that are as old as the human race itself, there is no "fountain of youth" to ward off aging and death. Still, there is a solution to many of the problems that undermine sound health. In a word, that solution is prevention. Prevention, which includes health promotion and education, saves lives, improves the quality of life, and in the long run, saves money.

In the United States, organized public health activities and preventive medicine have a long history. Important milestones in this country or foreign breakthroughs adopted in the United States include the improvement of sanitary procedures and the development of pasteurized milk in the late 19th century and the introduction in the mid-20th century of effective vaccines against polio, measles, German measles, mumps, and other once-rampant diseases. Internationally, organized public health efforts began on a wide-scale basis with the International Sanitary Conference of 1851, to which 12 nations sent representatives. The World Health Organization, founded in 1948, continues these efforts under the aegis of the United Nations, with particular emphasis on combating communicable diseases and the training of health care workers.

Despite these accomplishments, much remains to be done in the field of prevention. For too long, we have had a medical care system that is science- and technology-based, focused, essentially, on illness and mortality. It is now patently obvious that both the social and the economic costs of such a system are becoming insupportable.

Implementing prevention—and its corollaries, health education and promotion—is the job of several groups of people.

First, the medical and scientific professions need to continue basic scientific research, and here we are making considerable progress. But increased concern with prevention will also have a decided impact on how primary care doctors practice medicine. With a shift to health-based rather than morbidity-based medicine, the role of the "new physician" will include a healthy dose of patient education.

Second, practitioners of the social and behavioral sciences—psychologists, economists, city planners—along with lawyers, business leaders, and government officials—must solve the practical and ethical dilemmas confronting us: poverty, crime, civil rights, literacy, education, employment, housing, sanitation, environmental protection, health care delivery systems, and so forth. All of these issues affect public health.

Third is the public at large. We'll consider that very important group in a moment.

Fourth, and the linchpin in this effort, is the public health profession—doctors, epidemiologists, teachers—who must harness the professional expertise of the first two groups and the common sense and cooperation of the third, the public. They must define the problems statistically and qualitatively and then help us set priorities for finding the solutions.

To a very large extent, improving those statistics is the responsibility of every individual. So let's consider more specifically what the role of the individual should be and why health education is so important to that role. First, and most obvious, individuals can protect themselves from illness and injury and thus minimize their need for professional medical care. They can eat nutritious food; get adequate exercise; avoid tobacco, alcohol, and drugs; and take prudent steps to avoid accidents. The proverbial "apple a day keeps the doctor away" is not so far from the truth, after all.

Second, individuals should actively participate in their own medical care. They should schedule regular medical and dental checkups. Should they develop an illness or injury, they should know when to treat themselves and when to seek professional help. To gain the maximum benefit from any medical treatment that they do require, individuals must become partners in that treatment. For instance, they should understand the effects and side effects of medications. I counsel young physicians that there is no such thing as too much information when talking with patients. But the corollary is the patient must know enough about the nuts and bolts of the healing process to understand what the doctor is telling him or her. That is at least partially the patient's responsibility.

Education is equally necessary for us to understand the ethical and public policy issues in health care today. Sometimes individuals will encounter these issues in making decisions about their own treatment or that of family members. Other citizens may encounter them as jurors in medical malpractice cases. But we all become involved, indirectly, when we elect our public officials, from school board members to the president. Should surrogate parenting be legal? To what extent is drug testing desirable, legal, or necessary? Should there be public funding for family planning, hospitals, various types of medical research, and other medical care for the indigent? How should we allocate scant technological resources, such as kidney dialysis and organ transplants? What is the proper role of government in protecting the rights of patients?

What are the broad goals of public health in the United States today? In 1980, the Public Health Service issued a report aptly entitled *Promoting Health—Preventing Disease: Objectives for the Nation.* This report expressed its goals in terms of mortality and in terms of intermediate goals in education and health improvement. It identified 15 major concerns: controlling high blood pressure; improving family planning; improving pregnancy care and infant health; increasing the rate of immunization; controlling sexually transmitted diseases; controlling the presence of toxic agents and radiation in the environment; improving occupational safety and health; preventing accidents; promoting water fluoridation and dental health; controlling infectious diseases; decreasing smoking; decreasing alcohol and drug abuse; improving nutrition; promoting physical fitness and exercise; and controlling stress and violent behavior.

For healthy adolescents and young adults (ages 15 to 24), the specific goal was a 20% reduction in deaths, with a special focus on motor vehicle injuries and alcohol and drug abuse. For adults (ages 25 to 64), the aim was 25% fewer deaths, with a concentration on heart attacks, strokes, and cancers.

Smoking is perhaps the best example of how individual behavior can have a direct impact on health. Today, cigarette smoking is recognized as the single most important preventable cause of death in our society. It is responsible for more cancers and more cancer deaths than any other known agent; is a prime risk factor for heart and blood vessel disease, chronic bronchitis, and emphysema; and is a frequent cause of complications in pregnancies and of babies born prematurely, underweight, or with potentially fatal respiratory and cardiovascular problems.

Since the release of the Surgeon General's first report on smoking in 1964, the proportion of adult smokers has declined substantially, from 43% in 1965 to 30.5% in 1985. Since 1965, 37 million people have quit smoking. Although there is still much work to be done if we are to become a "smoke-free society," it is heartening to note that public health and public education efforts—such as warnings on cigarette packages and bans on broadcast advertising—have already had significant effects.

In 1835, Alexis de Tocqueville, a French visitor to America, wrote, "In America the passion for physical well-being is general." Today, as then, health and fitness are front-page items. But with the greater scientific and technological resources now available to us, we are in a far stronger position to make good health care available to everyone. And with the greater technological threats to us as we approach the 21st century, the need to do so is more urgent than ever before. Comprehensive information about basic biology, preventive medicine, medical and surgical treatments, and related ethical and public policy issues can help you arm yourself with the knowledge you need to be healthy throughout your life.

FOREWORD

Dale C. Garell, M.D.

Advances in our understanding of health and disease during the 20th century have been truly remarkable. Indeed, it could be argued that modern health care is one of the greatest accomplishments in all of human history. In the early 20th century, improvements in sanitation, water treatment, and sewage disposal reduced death rates and increased longevity. Previously untreatable illnesses can now be managed with antibiotics, immunizations, and modern surgical techniques. Discoveries in the fields of immunology, genetic diagnosis, and organ transplantation are revolutionizing the prevention and treatment of disease. Modern medicine is even making inroads against cancer and heart disease, two of the leading causes of death in the United States.

Although there is much to be proud of, medicine continues to face enormous challenges. Science has vanquished diseases such as smallpox and polio, but new killers, most notably AIDS, confront us. Moreover, we now victimize ourselves with what some have called "diseases of choice," or those brought on by drug and alcohol abuse, bad eating habits, and mismanagement of the stresses and strains of contemporary life. The very technology that is doing so much to prolong life has brought with it previously unimaginable ethical dilemmas related to issues of death and dying. The rising cost of health care is a matter of central concern to us all. And violence in the form of automobile accidents, homicide, and suicide remains the major killer of young adults.

In the past, most people were content to leave health care and medical treatment in the hands of professionals. But since the 1960s, the consumer of medical care—that is, the patient—has assumed an increasingly central role in the management of his or her own health. There has also been a new emphasis placed on prevention: People are recognizing that their own actions can help prevent many of the conditions that have caused death and disease in the past. This accounts for the growing commitment to good nutrition and regular exercise, for the increasing number of people who are choosing not to smoke, and for a new moderation in people's drinking habits.

People want to know more about themselves and their own health. They are curious about their body: its anatomy, physiology, and biochemistry. They want to keep up with rapidly evolving medical technologies and procedures. They are willing to educate themselves about common disorders and diseases so that they can be full partners in their own health care.

THE ENCYCLOPEDIA OF HEALTH is designed to provide the basic knowledge that readers will need if they are to take significant responsibility for their own health. It is also meant to serve as a frame of reference for further study and exploration. The encyclopedia is divided into five subsections: The Healthy Body; The Life Cycle; Medical Disorders & Their Treatment; Psychological Disorders & Their Treatment; and Medical Issues. For each topic covered by the encyclopedia, we present the essential facts about the relevant biology; the symptoms, diagnosis, and treatment of common diseases and disorders; and ways in which you can prevent or reduce the severity of health problems when that is possible. The encyclopedia also projects what may lie ahead in the way of future treatment or prevention strategies.

The broad range of topics and issues covered in the encyclopedia reflects that human health encompasses physical, psychological, social, environmental, and spiritual well-being. Just as the mind and the body are inextricably linked, so, too, is the individual an integral part of the wider world that comprises his or her family, society, and environment. To discuss health in its broadest aspect it is necessary to explore the many ways in which it is connected to such fields as law, social science, public policy, economics, and even religion. And so, the encyclopedia is meant to be a bridge between science, medical technology, the world at large, and you. I hope that it will inspire you to pursue in greater depth particular areas of interest and that you will take advantage of the suggestions for further reading and the lists of resources and organizations that can provide additional information.

CHAPTER ONE

THE SPEAKING ANIMAL

A wealthy Florida realtor suffered a stroke that robbed him of his ability to speak. Although he could understand what others said to him and was still able to write, his speech was so severely hampered that he sometimes said no when he meant to say yes. As noted in the book *The ABC's of Language & Linguistics*, by Curtis W. Hayes, Jacob Ornstein, and William W. Gage, the unhappy man once wrote, "Believe me, I'd give all my property and savings if I could only talk again."

Speech is a complex and remarkable form of communication. Although some might argue that writing is more vital to *Homo sapiens'* place in the world, it can be pointed out that several civilizations have existed without the written word—the Inuit of Alaska for one—but there have been none without speech.

A common example of the importance of speech can be found among immigrants and travelers who do not know the local language. They cannot ask directions or understand basic conversations, and it is a struggle for them just to get the basics of life—food and a place to sleep. Even the basic sounds of the new language may be difficult for the visitors to pronounce.

Despite the vital nature of speech, however, people rarely give a second thought to the intricate process behind it. In most situations a person simply has an idea, and almost instantaneously, the words expressing that thought come rolling effortlessly off of his or her tongue. Speaking is, however, the most rapid and complex physical activity that humans perform. In the moment between thought and speech, a person has to select a few key words from the thousands he or she knows, arrange them correctly, and make sure all the word endings and verb tenses agree. The word plan must then be transformed into a series of commands to the body's muscles to produce the sounds of speech.

THE COMPONENTS OF SPEECH

Speech scientists, known as *linguists*, divide the English language into 47 different sounds, called *phonemes*. A phoneme is the smallest unit of sound that differentiates one word from another and is the smallest divisible unit of language. In a sense phonemes are like atoms, but instead of combining to form molecules, they form words. Phonemes are signified by putting a letter or symbol between two slash marks. The word *bet* is made up of three phonemes: \b\, \E\, and \t\. By changing one phoneme, bet can become bit, bed, pet, set, bat, or bell.

Someone speaking fairly rapid English uses between 20 and 30 phonemes per second. Each phoneme requires a slightly different configuration of the vocal tract (nasal cavity, oral cavity, and *pharynx*).

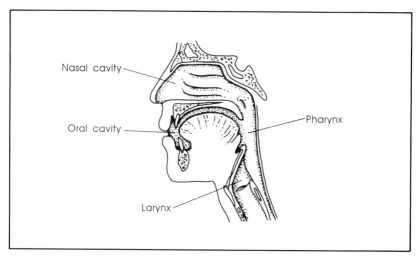

The human vocal tract is uniquely suited to speech.

In addition, the lips, tongue, jaw, rib cage, and vocal folds must all move to produce each phoneme, actions involving about 100 different muscles. Linguist E. H. Lenneberg has estimated that individual nerves fire 140,000 times per second to move the muscles involved in speech. Yet even mentally disabled children only three or four years of age can speak. French philosopher René Descartes observed that every human being appears to possess adequate intelligence to communicate through words.

THE ONLY TALKER

Along with the ability to make complex tools, speech separates humankind from the rest of the animal kingdom. If exposed to talking adults, almost all children learn easily and naturally how to speak. Speaking actually involves two distinct steps. First, the brain must convert ideas into words and arrange them in the proper order. This is the basis of language. The second step involves the physical movements that produce the sounds of speech, the vehicle for language. Speech production will be covered in Chapter Four.

French philosopher René Descartes observed that all human beings, no matter what their level of intelligence, are capable of learning language.

Language

In a broad sense language can be defined as the words used in communication, their pronunciation, and the rules needed to combine them. However, in a classic 1960 *Scientific American* article entitled "The Origin of Speech," linguist Charles F. Hockett went further, listing 13 different features of language. Many of the features, such as the use of vocal sounds, are not unique to human communication. But four of them he attributed solely to people.

One feature is the *duality of patterning*, which refers to the fact that humans combine a small pool of sounds, such as the 47 phonemes of English, to form a vast stock of words. Most other animals have a limited repertoire of sounds, each one of which has a specific meaning and cannot be combined with another sound to form anything new.

A second feature is the use of *displaced speech*, which involves the discussion of something that is not in the immediate vicinity, whether it is an uncle in Boise or a party next door. Bees use some displaced communication when they direct other bees to distant flowers containing nectar, but almost all other animals communicate only about things that are currently happening nearby.

A third distinctive characteristic is *traditional* or *cultural transmission*. Humans learn language from their parents or other adults, so that the knowledge is passed from generation to generation. Most other forms of animal communication appear to be inherited. Although some birds appear to learn the fine details of their calls, birds raised in isolation will still sing. Humans do not speak unless they can imitate others.

A fourth uniquely human feature of language is *productivity*. Humans can use existing words to produce an essentially infinite variety of sentences to express their thoughts and ideas. This opportunity for unbounded creativity is probably the most extraordinary characteristic of human language.

How do people acquire language? The 17th-century philosopher John Locke believed that the human mind begins as a blank slate. Understanding and knowledge are inscribed on the slate as a result of one's experiences, especially those gained through the physical senses of touch, smell, hearing, sight, and taste. According to Locke, language is just one of the areas of knowledge inscribed on the slate. Harvard psychologist B. F. Skinner put forward a similar idea. His 1959 book *Verbal Behavior* described language as a set of habits built up over the years. Based upon his work with rats and pigeons, Skinner stated that humans could learn language through what he called *operant conditioning*, a form of education using trial, error, and reward.

More popular, however, is the belief that humans possess an innate ability to learn language. Noam Chomsky, the most prominent linguist of the past 30 years, is an advocate of this view. He believes that as people learn language, existing switches in the brain are triggered. In the late 1950s he used logic and mathematical principles to develop a set of rules that could generate grammatical sentences. Using this system, Chomsky showed that language is much more complicated than most people had previously believed. He argues that language is too complex for children to learn as quickly as they do unless they are born with some innate capacity for it.

Harvard psychologist B. F. Skinner showed how animal behavior can be controlled through reinforcement. Here, pigeons learn to receive food by pressing controls in the Skinner Box. The scientist believed that language also is acquired through reinforcement.

Learning To Talk

When they are first born, all babies, including deaf ones, babble. Those who cannot hear eventually stop and become mute, but those who do hear people around them begin imitating the adult speech sounds. Although some babies take longer than others to learn to speak, most follow a broad, but consistent, pattern. Babies typically say their first word sometime near the end of their first year. They begin with one word at a time, then move on to two-word phrases. Next they begin what is known as *telegraphic speech*, longer sentences lacking plurals, tenses, prepositions, and other refinements of grammar. They then learn tenses and helper verbs, followed by plurals and negative structures. Most grammar is learned by the time children are 5 years old, with basic refinements continuing until the age of 10. Up until about age eight, children are also developing the physical skills necessary to properly pronounce all the sounds of a language.

Intelligence appears to have no effect on the age at which a baby begins speaking, and there also seems to be no way to speed up the learning process. Parents who try hard to teach their children to talk will do no better than those who allow youngsters to learn simply by picking up what those around them are saying. Yet as long as a child is exposed to people who speak and is allowed to practice, he or she will almost always learn to talk. There does, however, appear to be a critical period, ending at puberty, after which children find it much more difficult, if not impossible, to learn language.

Isabelle, the daughter of a deaf-mute, spent most of her first six and a half years in a darkened room. When finally released, the youngster could make only croaking sounds. Still within the critical period, however, she made remarkable progress, learning in two years the language skills it takes most children six years to acquire. Genie, on the other hand, was 14 when she was rescued from a father who confined her to a small room and punished her if she made noise. Having passed the onset of puberty with no language skills, she learned to speak in a rudimentary fashion but progressed more slowly than children normally do, and she failed to learn many of the basic concepts of language.

ORIGINS AND EVOLUTION OF SPEECH AND LANGUAGE

How can humankind do what other species apparently cannot? The answers are found in the brain and vocal tract. The complexity of the human brain allows thoughts to become language, and the human vocal tract has a unique shape that enables human beings to produce a wider range of sounds than can their closest relatives, the apes. The *larynx*, or voice box, is lower in the human throat than it is in an ape's. This makes the vocal tract a better sound chamber and places the tongue in a position that permits it to shape outgoing sounds more effectively. As a result, humans can create sounds such as \ u \ (good), \ i \ (free), and \ a \ (father), which apes cannot.

At first glance, however, the human vocal tract seems to have been an evolutionary step in the wrong direction, one that would decrease chances of survival. The lowered larynx increases the chances of choking on food. In other primates the pharynx, the muscular tube

ARTICULATE APES

Although it is true that speech separates humankind from other creatures, there have been arguments, spurred by efforts with chimpanzees and gorillas, that other animals can learn language. After years of research, scientists have had varying degrees of success in teaching other members of the animal kingdom to communicate with people.

Around the beginning of the 20th century, researchers began trying to teach apes to speak, but with poor results. In experiments carried out during the 1940s and 1950s, a chimp named Vicki apparently did manage to talk, but the animal learned to say only four basic words: mama, papa, up, and cup. The main stumbling block in such research has been that the anatomy of nonhuman primates is not adequate to form many of the speech sounds that people regularly make. Scientists have also tried to communicate with dolphins, which are very intelligent animals, but language experiments with them have not proved successful. "On the question as to whether dolphins have a language. . . ," psychologist John Morton wrote, "they are going to extraordinary lengths to conceal the fact from us."

Researchers have had better results teaching sign language to the great apes, humankind's closest relatives in the animal kingdom. Part of the reason is that these creatures are also keenly intelligent. For example, the gorilla Koko, who was formerly under study at Stanford University and now is at the Gorilla Foundation in California, attained scores ranging between 85 and 95 on an IQ test for which the average human score is 100. Sign-language experiments have been carried out with Koko as well as with several chimpanzees, including Washoe, who is currently at Central Washington University in Washington State.

Using hand signals found in the American Sign Language for the deaf, as well as magnetized symbols stuck to a board, researchers have succeeded in training the apes to understand and use anywhere from 100 to more than 300 symbols. Evidence suggests that the animals used these to communicate in ways considered to be reserved primarily for humans. Washoe, for example, appears to have referred to a swan by combining two words—*water* and *bird*. Some have questioned this finding, however, because it

Research involving great apes suggests that this group of animals is capable of acquiring language. Humans, however, still appear to be the only creature capable of consistently learning and employing this complex form of communication.

could be that Washoe was merely using each word to point out a separate feature—the swan and the body of water it occupied— instead of referring to the bird alone.

Washoe reportedly practiced cultural transmission when she taught a young chimp some of the signs she had learned. The primates have also used displaced "speech" to refer to objects not currently in their presence. Koko once even initiated a conversation to apologize for her nasty behavior several days earlier. Koko's achievements led her trainer, Penny Patterson, to remark that "language is no longer the exclusive domain of Man." The debate is far from set-

tled, however. Claiming that apes can acquire language because they learn simple signs, said Noam Chomsky, is like saying humans can fly because they can jump.

In addition, the primates involved in these studies appear to lack any true sense of grammar, and none have used their learned vocabulary to produce a great many new words. Plus, even if Koko or Washoe can be said to have acquired language, no ape has created the same complex form of communication outside the laboratory. Humans seem to be the only animal capable of consistently, and almost universally, learning and employing all the features of language.

Linguist Noam Chomsky suggested that humans have an innate ability to learn language.

containing the larynx, can rise like a periscope past the opening of the mouth and connect directly to the nasal cavity. In this position food travels around the pharynx and directly into the *esophagus*, the muscular tube leading to the stomach, so that food never has a chance to enter the pharynx and block breathing. In humans, the entrance to the pharynx does not rise up out of the way, which means that food must pass over the pharyngeal entrance on its way to the esophagus. As a result, food can slip down the wrong tube, block the pharynx, and choke a person, sometimes fatally.

Even so, the advantage of the lowered larynx, the physical ability to produce the highly varied and complex sounds of vocal communication, appears to outweigh the increased danger of choking. Vocal language allows for communication in a wider variety of circumstances than either gestures or a limited number of vocal calls do. Through speech, people can communicate at night and send complex messages over long distances and in areas of poor visibility. Vocal communication also frees the hands for other tasks, such as making and using tools. In addition, speech is an efficient method of transmitting information about either present, past, or future events and helps groups cooperate and work together in hunting or other endeavors.

It is not known exactly when the ancestors of humans acquired the ability to talk, although it clearly happened sometime after they dropped from the trees and began walking on two feet. Examinations of ancient human skeletons show little in terms of vocal tract development because most of the tract is made of soft tissue that quickly decomposes. Nonetheless, the recent discovery of a *hyoid bone*, the only bone in the modern human vocal tract, indicates that Neanderthals may have been able to speak as far back as 60,000 years ago.

Most anthropologists believe that a larger brain and the ability to speak developed together. The *gestural* theory, for example, suggests that when early humans began walking on two feet, their hands were freed, allowing them to manufacture and use tools. During the manufacturing process, the theory goes on to propose, material for the tool was usually manipulated by the left hand and fashioned with the

Children learn to speak by listening to others and practicing what they hear.

right. Those people with a more agile right hand could shape better tools and use them more easily, and that meant an increased chance of survival. The right hand is controlled by the left side of the brain, which is where speech centers for most people are located. A nimble right hand, therefore, may have meant that the left side of an individual's brain was better developed than that of other people, and as a result, that he or she had a better capacity for language as well.

Language helps humans to think by allowing them to define ideas. By expressing a thought, a person can examine it and correct or refine it. Language also helps to put ideas in a form that can be better held in the memory. However, there is controversy concerning the relationship between thought and language. Some believe that 18th-century lexicographer Samuel Johnson was correct when he said, "Language is the dress of thought." Others, however, believe the 19th-century poet Percy Bysshe Shelley was correct when he wrote, "He [God] gave men speech, and speech created thought."

CHAPTER TWO

THE BRAIN: SOURCE OF LANGUAGE

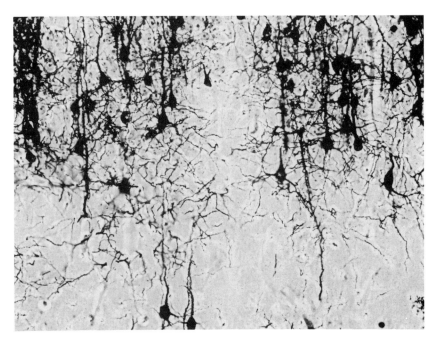

Billions of nerve cells are arranged into a complex network forming the human brain.

The human ability to speak hinges on a unique vocal tract and a powerful brain. The vocal tract, with its lowered larynx and flexible tongue, gives humans the physical means to produce the complex sounds that constitute speech. It is in the brain, however, that ideas arise, and it is also the brain that chooses and arranges words to express those ideas before sending commands through *neurons* (nerve cells) to the vocal tract muscles. The brain, therefore, is where language truly originates.

Studying the brain's relationship to language, however, has proven to be a particularly difficult challenge. Researchers have learned how the vocal tract works because they can see its physical movements and discern the effects. The brain, on the other hand, has no moving parts. Although modern techniques can provide information about electrical activity in the brain, this activity does not indicate the steps the brain takes to convert an idea into a sentence. Ethical considerations have prevented scientists from trying the same experiments on human brains that they perform on laboratory animals. However, by studying the neural effects of illness and accident, scientists have learned something about the way in which the brain operates. They have found, for example, that some areas of the brain appear to perform specific language and speech functions. Moreover, by carefully observing the way people speak and misspeak, researchers have learned how humans plan phrases and choose words to express their thoughts.

PHYSIOLOGY OF THE NERVOUS SYSTEM

The body's nervous system comprises the brain and spinal cord, as well as neurons going to almost every part of the body. The brain and spinal cord are referred to as the *central nervous system*, while the rest of the network forms the *peripheral nervous system*.

The nervous system contains billions of neurons. Minute electrical impulses travel along these cells, delivering messages to different parts of the body or brain. The neuron has a central cell body with two types of specialized branchlike extensions: *dendrites*, which receive impulses, and *axons*, which transmit them.

Chemicals called *neurotransmitters* carry messages from one nerve cell to another across a gap called the *synapse*. *Efferent neurons*, or *motor neurons*, carry impulses from the brain to different muscles. These impulses act as commands, telling muscles to contract. *Afferent neurons*, or *sensory neurons*, carry impulses from all regions of the body to the brain. These signals deliver information concerning heat, pressure, or pain. A *nerve* (as opposed to a complete nerve cell) is a bundle of axon fibers connecting the central nervous system and a

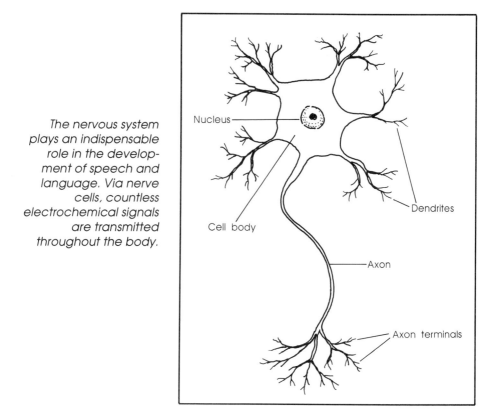

The nervous system plays an indispensable role in the development of speech and language. Via nerve cells, countless electrochemical signals are transmitted throughout the body.

peripheral part of the body, such as an arm or leg. The nerve can contain motor, sensory, or both kinds of fibers.

The brain itself can be divided into three structures. The *brain stem* sits at the base of the skull, atop the spinal column. It controls most of the *autonomic functions*, those housekeeping activities such as heartbeat, breathing, and temperature control that are vital but largely unconscious. The *cerebellum*, behind the brain stem, senses a person's physical location in space and helps coordinate the muscle commands that originate in the higher brain, or *cerebrum*. The cerebrum makes up the largest part of the brain. Its convoluted surface tissue, the *cerebral cortex*, is the site of complex, conscious thoughts. The cerebrum has two halves, or *hemispheres*, which are connected by a bundle of nerve fibers called the *corpus callosum*.

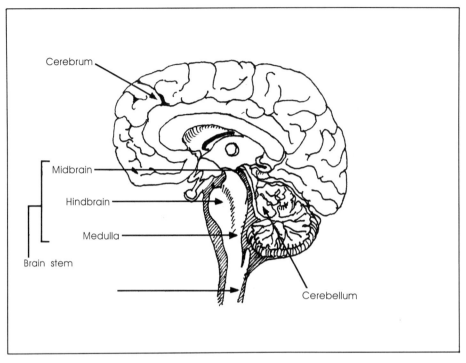

Cerebrum

Midbrain

Hindbrain

Medulla

Brain stem

Cerebellum

The structure and meaning of language are formed in the brain.

SPECIALIZED BRAIN FUNCTIONS

Autopsies, medical examinations of dead people, provided some of the earliest information about areas within the cerebrum devoted to specific tasks. By examining brains taken from corpses, physicians could sometimes associate various speech problems with damage to particular areas of the brain. Brain damage often results from a blow to the head or a *stroke*. During a stroke, blood vessels in the brain burst or are blocked, preventing blood from carrying oxygen and nutrients to cells beyond the damaged area. As a result, portions of the brain die.

Broca's Area

In 1861 Parisian physician Paul Broca examined the brains of two deceased patients who had suffered severe speech defects. Both patients had significant brain damage in an area just in front of and slightly above the left ear. This area came to be known as *Broca's area.* It appears to play a crucial role in the physical production of speech. Damage there often causes people to speak slowly, with great effort and poor pronunciation, and in grammatically incomplete sentences. Norman Geschwind, in a 1979 *Scientific American* article entitled "Specializations of the Human Brain," quoted a person suffering from this type of problem responding to a question about a dental appointment: "Yes . . . Monday . . . Dad and Dick . . . Wednesday . . . nine

Researchers Paul Broca (left) and Carl Wernicke (right) both discovered areas of the brain that influence speech.

o'clock . . . ten o'clock . . . doctors . . . and teeth." This condition, called *Broca's aphasia*, is a frustrating problem for its victims. Patients understand questions asked of them and seem to know the idea they want to express but cannot get the words out.

Wernicke's Area

In 1874, German medical investigator Carl Wernicke examined the brains of former patients who had suffered a problem associated more with comprehension and language than with speech production. These people had spoken fluidly and with no pronunciation difficulties. However, their sentences often had little meaning attached to them, and sometimes the words themselves were nonsensical. Wernicke's autopsies also revealed brain damage on the left side, but this time behind the left ear, a spot farther back than Broca's area. That location is now called *Wernicke's area*, and damage there frequently causes *Wernicke's aphasia*. It is, again, difficult for a patient suffering from this condition to make sense, and when he or she does, it often takes a long time and many words to do so. Geschwind quotes a Wernicke's aphasiac trying to describe a picture of two boys stealing cookies behind a woman's back. The patient said, "Mother is away here working her work to get her better, but when she's looking the two boys looking in the other part. She's working another time."

Penfield and Roberts

In the 1950s Canadian surgeons Wilder Penfield and Lamar Roberts used direct electrical stimulation of the brain to confirm the roles of Wernicke's and Broca's areas. Their purpose was to ensure that while attempting to treat epileptic seizures by removing brain tissue, they did not also remove tissue associated with speech. Because the brain has no sensory nerve cells and feels no pain, the researchers could look for the speech areas while operating on fully conscious patients. The two surgeons would remove a piece of the skull and then apply a tiny electrical current to different parts of the cerebral cortex. Stimulation of Broca's and Wernicke's areas interfered with the production and comprehension of speech. (Penfield and Roberts also found a small area near the top of the brain, called the *superior speech cortex*, that plays a lesser role in the motor functions of speech.)

The work of Broca, Wernicke, Penfield, and Roberts indicated that two areas on the left side of the brain play vital roles in speech and language. Damage to the opposite side of the brain normally causes no similar speech problems. (It has since been discovered that a small minority of people do have speech centers on the right side of the brain.)

Some scientists, however, question the role of both Broca's and Wernicke's areas. They believe that damage or electrical stimulation only show what happens when those areas of the brain are not working but do not reveal the function they perform when they are operating properly. These researchers also suggest that other areas make a sig-

Broca's area and Wernicke's area are both located in the left hemisphere of the brain. Damage to either section can result in the communication disorder known as aphasia.

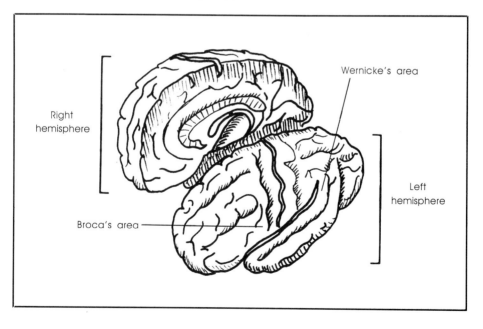

31

nificant contribution to speech and language as well, particularly since damage to either Broca's area or Wernicke's area does not always result in aphasia.

SLIPS OF THE BRAIN

While these studies provide some information about speech and language centers in the brain, they tell nothing about the process of formulating sentences; that is, how people choose and arrange words to express their ideas. Only by listening closely to the way in which people speak have researchers learned some of the steps the brain takes when stringing words together to express a thought. The errors speakers sometimes make during these steps are especially instructive, providing insight into the brain's linguistic process.

People make two basic kinds of mistakes when they speak. These are known as *selection* and *assemblage* errors. Selection errors occur when a person chooses the wrong word for a particular sentence. Assemblage mistakes happen when a speaker has selected all the right sounds but misplaces words or parts of words within the sentence. Each type of error is really a slip of the brain rather than a slip of the tongue, and both tell something different about the way humans plan speech. (Most of the following examples are taken from Jean Aitchison's book on psycholinguistics, *The Articulate Mammal*.)

William A. Spooner, an English clergyman and dean of Oxford's New College in the late 19th century, is infamous for the assemblage errors—now called *spoonerisms*—he allegedly made. Instead of admonishing students for missing his history lectures and wasting the school term, he supposedly told them, "You hissed all my mystery lectures" and "have tasted the whole worm." Although the man did exist and was known to misspeak, his famous utterances are somewhat suspect because they always seem to make sense and affect only initial sounds. Assemblage errors can also occur among noninitial sounds, such as in the phrase "a cop of cuffee." The problem can occasionally involve full words, too, as when a person says, "I can't help the man if it's deluded," instead of "I can't help it if the man's deluded."

Research by Canadian surgeon Wilder Penfield helped confirm the importance of both Broca's area and Wernicke's area in the production of speech.

A more common form of assemblage error is *anticipation*, which occurs when a person utters a word or sound too early. Instead of saying that he or she is about to make an "important point," a person might anticipate the "oi" sound and say "impoitant point." Words can also be anticipated, as in the phrase "when you buy the laundry," instead of "when you take the laundry, buy me some cigarettes." In other cases, people sometimes repeat sounds, saying a "tall toy" instead of a "tall boy." These mistakes most frequently occur close together, within a single phrase. This suggests that people plan the entire phrase before saying it, choosing and arranging several words at a time and then occasionally misassembling the parts.

When does a person plan a phrase? Researchers have gained insight into this question by looking not at words but at the gaps between them. During spontaneous speech a person spends about 40% to 50% of the time saying nothing. Pauses to take a breath account for only about 5%

of all the silent time and tend to occur at grammatical boundaries, such as between sentences or clauses. Ninety-five percent of the silence during speech is of the "um . . . er" variety known as a *hesitation pause*. Although researchers disagree as to exactly when most of these pauses occur, they do agree that the pauses happen within clauses rather than between them, indicating that there is an overlap in the planning and production of clauses. People do not plan one clause, say it, then plan a second clause. Even as they begin to speak they are still planning the initial clause. Then, somewhere in the midst of speaking that first clause, they move on and begin planning the next. Hesitation pauses may serve as a rest stop between the planning stages.

Speech errors also demonstrate that planning is a complicated matter in which the material is first outlined in the speaker's mind. Researchers who have studied both transpositions and anticipations have learned that on the rare occasion when a person does cross a clause

Speaking mistakes attributed to British clergyman William A. Spooner came to be known as spoonerisms.

boundary with a mistake, the error always involves entire words that are transposed or anticipated, not sound segments. Mistakes with sound segments or word endings tend to occur within a phrase, indicating that people choose key words during the outline planning. When a wrong word is chosen or two words are transposed, both the mistaken word and the right word are almost always the same part of speech—noun, adjective, or adverb. This indicates that the basic structure of the sentence has been chosen even though the final selections have not been made.

Yet when words are misplaced or misspoken, the errors do not disrupt the intonation patterns. A person who says, "We'll go to taxi in a town," says it with the same intonation as a person saying, "We'll go to town in a taxi." This suggests that the speaker has already outlined the basic structure, or syntax, of a sentence, and that this structure stays the same even when the placement of the words is wrong. Key words, rough syntax (arrangement of words), and intonation patterns are put in place during the outline planning. Fitting the words together with the right auxiliary words and endings occurs later, during detailed planning.

How do people actually choose the words to express an idea? To answer this question, scientists designed an experiment that catches the brain in the process. In 1966 researchers R. Brown and D. McNeill read definitions of relatively uncommon words, then asked students to name each word being defined. In some cases the students immediately named the right word. Others went into what is called the "Tip-of-Tongue," or TOT, state in which they could almost recall the word. Brown and McNeill then asked the subjects several questions about the sought-after word. The students could provide quite a bit of information concerning the *semantics* (meaning) and *phonetics* (sound). In response to the definition of *sextant*, a navigational instrument, students came up with words such as astrolabe, compass, and protractor, all of which have related meanings. Others remembered that the word had two syllables and started with an S, coming up with such guesses as secant, sexton, and sextet. Words are apparently stored in the memory according to both sound and meaning.

People appear to retrieve words from memory through a method called *spreading activation*. Each stored word is linked to other words, both semantically and phonetically. The search for the appropriate word to express an idea presumably activates these associations, which spread throughout a person's stored vocabulary until the right word is found and retrieved. Even on occasions when the correct word cannot be located, many phonetically and semantically similar ones do come to mind.

CHAPTER THREE

ACOUSTICS

Sound technology has come a long way since the invention of this early phonograph.

Understanding the nature of sound is crucial to understanding speech and hearing. A speaker produces a stream of constantly changing sounds that travel through the air and cause parts of the listener's ear to vibrate. Those vibrations trigger nerve impulses that travel to the brain, where they are interpreted as messages with meaning. Sound is the link between speaker and listener. The subject dealing with the properties of sound is called *acoustics*.

WHAT IS SOUND?

Sound is a disturbance that travels through an elastic medium, most commonly air. However, it can also pass through other materials, such as water, the steel in railroad tracks, or the wood and plaster in walls. The disturbance in a medium is created by vibrating objects, such as guitar strings or vocal folds. The importance of a medium can be demonstrated by placing an alarm clock inside a jar. At first the alarm creates a sound that can be heard by a person standing nearby. As a vacuum pump sucks air out of the jar, however, the sound of the alarm weakens, then stops, even though the clapper is still hitting the alarm clock's bell. Without a medium, such as air, to transmit the disturbance, there is no sound. To understand how a disturbance travels through a medium, think of a stretched-out spring. If a person holds one end and gives it a sharp shove, it will compress some of the spring's coils, and that compression will travel down the length of the spring.

The disturbance called sound is an alternating sequence of high and low pressure, known as *compression* and *rarefaction* respectively. To

Sound waves are formed when groups of air molecules are alternately pushed together and pulled apart, forming areas of compression and rarefaction.

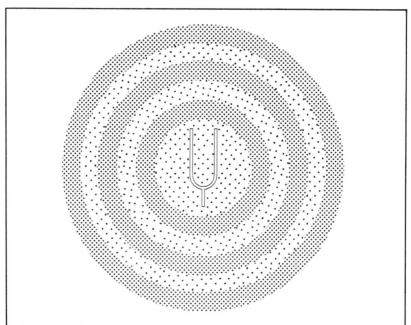

illustrate this concept, consider a tuning fork. When struck against something hard, the fork's tines vibrate back and forth, producing sound. As the two tines move outward to their widest position, they push air molecules together, creating an area of compression. When the tines move back toward each other, they leave behind an area of few molecules, creating rarefaction. Moving back and forth several hundred or thousand times per second, the tuning fork's tines create an alternating sequence of low- and high-pressure areas that travel outward from the fork. Again, it might be visualized by imagining a spring attached to the tuning fork. As the fork vibrates, it will alternately compress and stretch the spring, with those pushed and pulled areas moving in sequence down the spring's length. Yet even though the individual coils move back and forth, they return to their original spot once the disturbance has moved to the next group of coils. Air molecules do the same, moving back and forth as the sound disturbance travels through them but returning to their original position once the vibration has passed. This pattern of compression and rarefaction is called a *sound wave*.

Sound can be divided into two categories: *periodic* and *aperiodic*. Periodic sound is produced by an object that vibrates in a repetitive pattern, producing tones such as those made by musical instruments, a tuning fork, or a person saying "ah." Periodic sounds can be either *complex* or *pure*. Aperiodic sounds, in contrast, are produced by an object vibrating in no apparent pattern and do not contain tones. Instead, they are considered *noise* and include the sound of a single drumbeat, sandpaper scraping wood, or a person saying "sk," as in the word *sky*.

SIMPLE HARMONIC MOTION AND PURE TONES

A tuning fork produces a pure periodic tone through the uncomplicated, repetitive movement known as *simple harmonic motion*. The tines of the tuning fork move regularly back and forth between two extremes. The movements of a swing or a pendulum are other examples of simple harmonic motion.

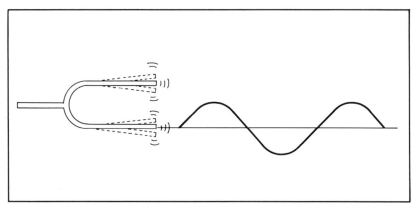

The shape of a simple sine wave can be seen in the motion of a vibrating tuning fork.

Waveform

A person can draw a graph describing simple harmonic motion by tying a pen to the end of a vibrating tuning fork and pulling a piece of paper beneath. The figure produced is a simple sine curve and can be described using uncomplicated mathematical formulas. This same curve can also be used to describe the air disturbance caused by sound as it moves past a point (see illustration). The horizontal axis represents time, and the vertical axis represents pressure. The spot where the horizontal and vertical axis intersect is the point of *equilibrium pressure*, that is, the pressure of undisturbed air. When an area of compression passes the chosen point in space, the curve climbs above the straight line on the drawing. As that area of compression moves on and is followed by an area of rarefaction, the line dips below the equilibrium pressure. All kinds of sound can be portrayed using waveforms, but most are irregular and more complex.

Different sounds produce differently shaped waves. Each sound can be analyzed by studying the characteristics of its waves. *Amplitude* and *frequency* are the two most commonly cited features of a sound wave, but *wavelength*, *period*, and *phase* are also important to understand.

Amplitude refers to the height of the curve or how far its peak is from equilibrium (not the distance from peak to the very bottom of the wave). For sound waves the amplitude measures pressure differences created by a vibrating object. People generally sense greater amplitude as louder sound (see Chapter Six), yet the pressure increases caused by sound disturbances are very small. For example, a normal voice creates a pressure increase of only about one millionth of an atmosphere. (An atmosphere is a unit of pressure equal to the air pressure at sea level, or 14.69 pounds per square inch.)

In a periodic wave, the frequency is the number of times a cycle repeats in a second, or how many waves pass a specific point in one second. Sound audible to human ears repeats itself anywhere from 20 to 20,000 times per second. Sound frequencies are often noted in *hertz* (Hz). One hertz is one repetition per second. Twenty thousand hertz means the cycle repeats 20,000 times per second. Generally, higher-frequency sounds are sensed as having a higher *pitch*.

Low-frequency sounds pass through and around obstacles much better than high-frequency sounds do. This can render someone speaking one room away from the listener unintelligible because the listener hears the low frequencies from the speaker's voice but not the high ones. It is also the reason why a person can hear the low bass frequencies of a loud stereo through the wall but not the high frequencies.

To describe the characteristics of sound, scientists use the concepts of amplitude, wavelength, period, and frequency. Figure (b) has a higher frequency than figure (a).

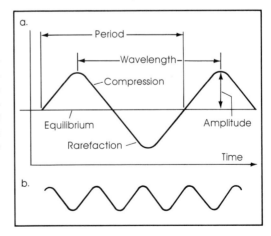

41

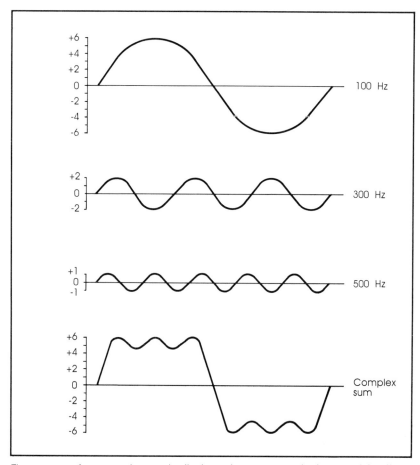

The wave of a complex periodic tone is composed of a combination of simple sine waves.

Nonetheless, low frequencies tend to sound weaker than the high ones do, something audio equipment manufacturers take into account when designing their products. Amplifiers give low frequencies a little extra boost in intensity, and the loudness switch on an amplifier adds still more kick.

Wavelength is the physical distance between repeating points on the wave. A person saying "ah" typically produces a tone of about 100 Hz. The wavelength of a 100-Hz tone can be figured by dividing the speed of sound in air by the frequency, or 100 Hz. If, for example, the speed of the sound wave is 1,130 feet per second (such speeds can vary according to the temperature and pressure of air), the 100-Hz tone has a wavelength of 11.3 feet.

The period of a wave is the time needed for its wavelength to pass a single point in space, making it the reciprocal of the wave's frequency. A 100-Hz tone, for example, has a period lasting one hundredth of a second. The higher the frequency, the shorter the wavelength and period.

To determine the phase of a simple sine wave send the wave through the air and pick a spot on that wave at any particular moment. The phase of the wave refers to whether it is in a state of compression or rarefaction at that point in space and time. Two waves in the same phase are compressed or rarefied at the same time.

Complex Tones

Pure tones are relatively rare in nature. Most periodic sounds are complex tones whose waveform is more complicated than the simple sine curve of a pure tone is. Although the waveform of a complex tone has many more fluctuations than that of a pure tone, it does repeat itself. French mathematician Jean-Baptiste-Joseph Fourier (1768–1830) showed that any repetitive, or periodic, function can be described as a combination of simple sine waves, each with a different frequency, amplitude, and phase.

Harmonics

All complex tones can be described as the sum of several pure tones, represented by simple harmonic curves. The pure tone components, however, cannot be just any curves. They must all have frequencies that are multiples of the lowest frequency component, known as the *fundamental frequency*. If the fundamental frequency is 500 Hz, the other components must have frequencies of 1,000 Hz, 1,500 Hz, 2,000 Hz, or some other multiple of 500. These higher-frequency tones are called *harmonics* of the fundamental frequency.

French mathematician Jean-Baptiste-Joseph Fourier (1768–1830) dissected complex waves into their simpler parts.

The pitch of a complex tone corresponds to its fundamental frequency, while the harmonics produce more subtle sound differences. Harmonics are responsible for the variations between one voice and another, and also for the sound differences between musical instruments. A guitar and a flute may produce a note with the same fundamental frequency, such as middle C, but their different harmonics give each its distinctive sound. In speech, the harmonics are also crucial in distinguishing different vowel sounds.

APERIODIC SOUNDS

Many sounds cannot be represented by periodic waves or by a mathematical formula. These aperiodic sounds do not produce tones. Most consonant sounds, such as "k," are aperiodic, as are the sounds of a book dropping on the ground or the wind blowing through the leaves of a tree.

RESONANCE

Every vibrating object has a *natural resonant frequency*. This is the frequency at which it will vibrate once set in motion and left alone. If a swing is pulled back and released, it will move back and forth at one frequency. Even as the swing completes shorter and shorter arcs, the time between peaks will remain the same, completing the same number of swings in a given time period. For the swing, the natural resonant frequency is dependent upon the length of the ropes holding it. Shorten the ropes and that frequency will be higher; lengthen them and it will

An acoustic resonator will vibrate at one or more frequencies, all of which are related to the size and shape of the air-filled container. Cellos and violins are among the instruments that produce sounds using acoustic resonance.

be lower. Similarly, each string on a guitar has a different resonant frequency, which is dependent upon the weight of the string and how tightly it is strung.

Should someone produce a sound at or near the natural resonant frequency of an object, the object will begin to vibrate. If, for example, a person sings a middle C note next to the middle C string of a piano, the string will vibrate. Similarly, if someone pushes a moving swing, the timing of the push makes a tremendous difference in the effect it has. The most effective way to push a swing is to shove it each time the swing reaches the top of its arc, so that the pushes coincide with the swing's natural resonant frequency. Pushing the swing before it reaches its peak would be less effective, sometimes even slowing the swing down. When vibrating an object, such as a pushed swing, the highest amplitude can be achieved by applying force at or near the natural resonant frequency.

Acoustic Resonance

Bodies of air also have natural resonant frequencies. Their volume is the primary determinant, but the shape of the space in which the air is enclosed also plays a role. Larger volumes of air generally have lower natural resonant frequencies. An enclosed body of air, known as an *acoustic resonator*, will amplify sounds at or near its natural resonant frequency and damp sounds that are far from it. To get an idea of how changes in the resonator can alter the natural resonant frequency, think of a bottle being filled with water. As the liquid climbs higher, the sound leaving the bottle rises in frequency. An acoustic resonator can have more than one natural resonant frequency. These devices are largely responsible for the different sounds of guitars, cellos, and bass fiddles. Each instrument has a different volume of air in its resonator and thus vibrates at different frequencies from the others. Acoustic resonance also plays an important role in the sounds created by the vocal folds and resonated in the vocal tract.

DECIBELS

Sound level, the magnitude of a sound, is measured in a unit known as the *decibel*. A decibel is one-tenth of a *bel*, named after Alexander Graham Bell, the inventor of the telephone and educator of the deaf. The symbol for decibel is dB.

The decibel scale is a logarithmic, or exponential, scale. On the more familiar linear scale—for example, the measurements along a ruler—each increment is equal to the next; the distance between one inch and two on a ruler is the same as the distance between two inches

Commonplace sounds measured in decibels

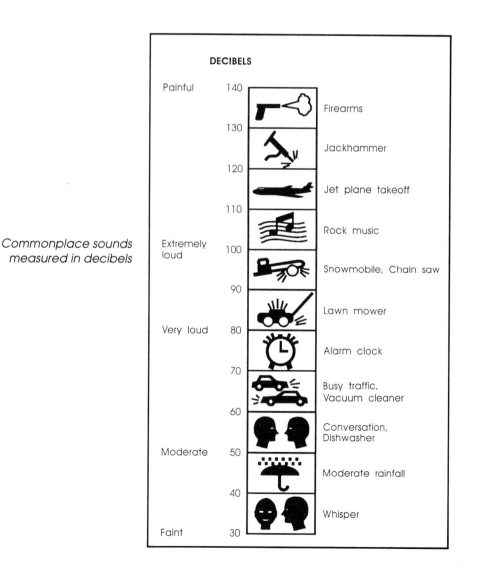

DECIBELS

Painful	140	Firearms
	130	Jackhammer
	120	Jet plane takeoff
	110	Rock music
Extremely loud	100	Snowmobile, Chain saw
	90	Lawn mower
Very loud	80	Alarm clock
	70	Busy traffic, Vacuum cleaner
	60	Conversation, Dishwasher
Moderate	50	Moderate rainfall
	40	Whisper
Faint	30	

and three. On a logarithmic scale, however, the increments grow increasingly large. The increments in the logarithmic decibel scale are based on exponents of 10. That means when a sound increases by 10 dB, the sound's intensity increases 10 times, but a 20-dB increase ups the intensity by 10^2, or 100 times. An increase of 30 dB lifts the intensity by 10^3, or 1,000 times. A 0-dB sound is just audible to most people. A 130-dB sound, the threshold of pain for most people, is 10^{13}, or 10 trillion times as intense.

One reason that the logarithmic scale is used is that the range of human hearing is so great that a linear scale would require using large, unwieldy numbers. The logarithmic scale provides a more manageable set of figures.

LOUDNESS

As previously mentioned, loudness is related to the intensity, or amplitude, of the sound wave. Generally, the greater the amplitude, the louder a sound is perceived to be. Increasing a sound by 3 dB doubles the intensity of a sound, but that difference is just barely noticeable to most people. Increasing a 1,000-Hz sound from 20 dB to 66 dB increases its intensity by 40,000 times, although most people perceive it as a 100-fold increase in loudness. Loudness is also influenced by the frequency of the sound wave. If two sounds have the same intensity but different frequencies, the one with the lower frequency will sound louder than the other. As sound intensity increases, however, frequency becomes less of a factor.

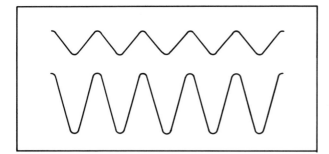

The higher the amplitude, or intensity, of a sound wave, the louder the sound is perceived.

PITCH

Pitch is the property of sound that can be described as higher and lower notes on a musical scale and is related to the fundamental frequency of a particular tone. Generally, the higher the frequency is, the higher the pitch. However, pitch can also be slightly affected by intensity. The pitch of a 300-Hz tone, for example, will lower as the intensity increases.

The ability to sense pitch varies widely from person to person. At one end of the scale are those people who are *tone deaf*. They can often distinguish between two notes played on a piano, but when asked to sing in the pitch being played, they usually produce a tone that bears little resemblance to the one they are trying to reproduce. At the other end of the talent scale are people with *perfect pitch*, an ability to hum any note named or to identify any that is played. The great composer Wolfgang Amadeus Mozart fell into this category. Scientists do not yet know the secret behind perfect pitch, although the skill does tend to run in families. There is also evidence that perfect pitch can be learned. In other cases, musicians have what is known as *relative pitch*, which allows them to identify tonal intervals, that is, how far apart two notes are on the musical scale.

The Doppler effect occurs as the source of sound waves passes the listener. As a speeding train approaches, for example, the waves crowd together, raising the sound's pitch. As the train moves farther away, there is a greater distance between the waves, and the pitch lowers.

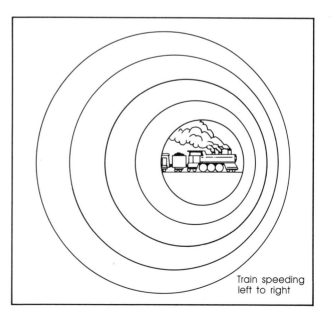

Train speeding left to right

Doppler Effect

Anyone listening to a moving car or train may have noticed that the vehicle seems to emit a higher-pitched sound when it is approaching and a lower-pitched sound after it has passed. This phenomenon is called the *Doppler effect*. As the vehicle moves rapidly closer, each sound wave has less distance to travel than the one before it. As a result, the sound waves begin to crowd each other, shortening the wavelengths reaching the listener's ear and producing a higher frequency and higher-pitched sound. After the vehicle has passed, each sound wave is emitted from a little farther away, effectively stretching out the waves, which in turn lowers both the frequency and the pitch.

Composer Wolfgang Amadeus Mozart possessed perfect pitch, allowing him to identify any musical note played.

CHAPTER FOUR

SPEECH PRODUCTION

Professional singers such as Whitney Houston can produce a variety of sounds ranging far across the musical scale.

Singers sometimes refer to their voice as a musical instrument, something to be played in much the same way other musicians use a guitar or piano. Indeed, operatic tenor Luciano Pavarotti and pop singer Whitney Houston both use their vocal instruments to produce sounds that range far across both ends of the musical scale. Yet in a way, describing the voice as an instrument is actually underestimating its abilities, because humans produce a greater variety of sounds than even the most sophisticated musical instrument. In addition to carrying a tune, singers can produce a complex stream of sounds that form the syllables, words, and sentences of language.

The human vocal system consists of three basic components: the lungs, larynx, and vocal tract. These originally served more limited purposes for humankind's ancestors: The lungs acted to take in oxygen and excrete carbon dioxide, the larynx worked as a valve to prevent unwanted objects from getting into the lungs, and the vocal tract was used as a passageway for food, liquid, and air. As humans developed the ability to speak, however, these organs took on additional functions.

The lungs are now the engine of speech, providing a steady stream of air that is converted into sound waves by vocal folds in the larynx. The vocal tract acts as an acoustic resonator that amplifies some sound-wave frequencies and muffles others, in addition to producing its own sounds.

The human vocal system consists of three basic components: the lungs, larynx, and vocal tract.

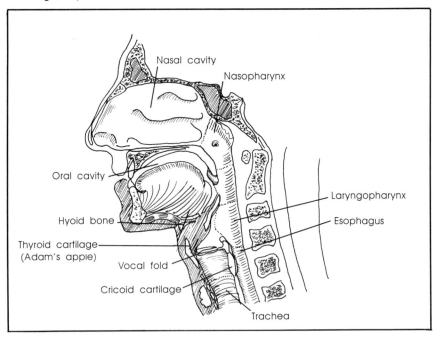

LUNGS

The lungs function like an accordion or bellows, possessing an outer frame that expands and contracts to force air in and out. Normal breathing is controlled by a part of the brain stem known as the *medulla oblongata*. When it senses that the body needs to expel carbon dioxide and take in oxygen, the brain signals muscles in the abdomen and rib cage, which then work to expand the rib cage and the lungs. Air rushes in to fill the lungs' larger volume.

To exhale, a person relaxes his or her muscles, allowing the rib cage and diaphragm to return to their resting positions, thus shrinking the lungs and squeezing out extra air. This happens an average of 12 to 20 times a minute, 24 hours a day, mostly without any conscious attention. During normal breathing a person inhales and exhales about half a quart of air at a time, spending a little more time exhaling than inhaling. During speech, however, a person communicating in English spends about 90% of the time exhaling because all English speech sounds are made by expelling air. The exhalation requires precise muscle control

By acting as a pump to draw in oxygen and expel carbon dioxide, the lungs provide a steady stream of air to fuel the production of sound waves.

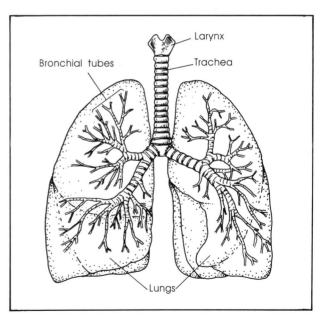

Larynx

Bronchial tubes

Trachea

Lungs

to prolong it and to determine the rate of air flow, which affects the pitch and volume of a person's voice. Breaths taken during speech average a little more than twice the volume of those taken during quiet breathing. In addition, people time their breaths according to the length of phrases and sentences to be uttered. For example, most people will say, "I want to go roller skating at the park this afternoon," instead of, "I want to go roller"—(pause, inhale)—"skating at the park this afternoon."

LARYNX

The larynx is an hourglass-shaped organ that sits at the top of the *trachea*, the tube that carries air up from the lungs. The narrow part of the hourglass, the vocal folds, vibrates during speech, converting the stream of air from the lungs into sound waves.

Four pieces of fibrous flexible tissue called *cartilage* form the larynx's framework. The *cricoid cartilage* forms the base on which the other three cartilages sit. The *thyroid cartilage* is a V-shaped shield that forms the front wall of the larynx. Men have a larger thyroid cartilage with a more sharply angled V, which creates the bulge in the neck called the *Adam's apple*. Two smaller, pyramid-shaped cartilages, known as *arytenoid cartilages*, sit on top of the cricoid cartilage, about half an inch apart at the back of the larynx.

The larynx is held in place by muscles that attach it to the horseshoe-shaped hyoid bone above and the *sternum* (breastbone) below. When a person swallows, some of these muscles contract to pull the larynx upward and forward, out of the way of food heading toward the back of the throat to the esophagus. That is why the Adam's apple can be seen moving upward during swallowing. The ability to bob up and down also allows the larynx to change the size of the vocal tract and, as a result, its natural resonant frequencies.

In 1741 a French scientist named Antoine Ferrein coined the term *vocal cords*, because he thought the larynx contained two strings that made noise by vibrating much like a guitar or piano string. Although this was not entirely accurate, the phrase stuck. In reality, however, the vocal cords, or as they are referred to in this book, vocal folds, include a pair of *vocal ligaments* and two *vocalis muscles*. The folds are attached side-by-side to the thyroid cartilage at the front of the larynx. They are also attached to the pyramid-shaped arytenoid cartilages located at the back of the larynx, and all four ligaments and muscles are covered by mucous membrane. When the vocal folds are at rest, there is a V-shaped gap between them known as the *glottis*. Muscles flex to rotate and push the arytenoid cartilages together, causing the vocal folds to touch from front to back.

In 1848 German researcher Johannes Müller removed the larynges (plural of larynx) from several cadavers. He attached strings to the cartilages to simulate the action of muscles and forced air through the larynx. His experiments disproved Ferrein's vibrating string theory and gave rise to the *myoelastic-aerodynamic theory of phonation*. This theory describes how muscle (myo) tension and flexibility combine with air movement (aerodynamics) to create audible puffs of air.

To produce sound through the larynx, a person exhales and at the same time flexes muscles that push the vocal folds together. As air is pushed up from the lungs and presses against the vocal folds, the folds

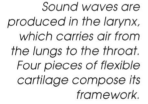

Sound waves are produced in the larynx, which carries air from the lungs to the throat. Four pieces of flexible cartilage compose its framework.

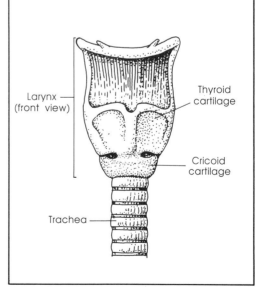

flap open and closed again and again. This is the same effect that occurs when a child imitates the putt-putt-putt sound of a motorboat by blowing air through his or her closed lips. During speech, air pressure builds up again, and the process repeats itself. During normal speech the vocal folds open and shut between 80 and 500 times a minute.

The opening and shutting of the vocal folds produces alternately compressed and rarefied (less dense) air, which forms the sound waves of the human voice. The faster the vocal folds vibrate, the higher the frequency of sound they produce. The rate of vocal fold vibration depends upon the muscle tension and the weight and length of the vocal folds, as well as the air pressure pushing against them. Men generally have longer and heavier vocal folds than women or children do, giving them lower voices.

VOCAL TRACT

The *supralaryngeal* (above the larynx) vocal tract functions both as a resonator of the sound produced in the larynx and as its own sound source. The shape of the cavity, or more importantly, the amount and distribution of the air inside it, determines its resonant frequencies. Those frequencies are altered as the throat, mouth, tongue, and nasal cavity change their shape. Sounds are produced in the vocal tract by constricting it to create hisses and bursts such as the sounds \ s \ and \ t \ .

The vocal folds, which are located in the larynx, are composed of muscles and ligaments. Air pushed up from the lungs causes the folds to vibrate, producing sound waves.

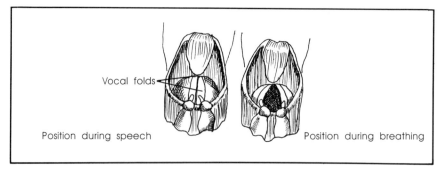

Vocal folds

Position during speech

Position during breathing

The pharynx is a tube of muscles connecting the back of the mouth and the nasal cavities with the trachea and esophagus. Humans can change the pharynx's shape by constricting muscles and by moving the tongue. Because the human larynx sits lower in the pharynx than in other animals, the pharynx is a larger, more effective resonating cavity.

The tongue, a large, rounded muscle, sits on the inside corner of the vocal tract, where the pharynx meets the mouth. The tongue dramatically changes the vocal tract's shape and resonant frequencies in two ways: by moving to different positions in the pharynx or mouth and by changing its own shape (for example, lifting or lowering the tip and curling the sides). The tongue is the most active part of the vocal tract and plays the biggest role in shaping speech sounds.

The lips and lower jaw are also important features of the oral cavity. The lips can lengthen or shorten the vocal tract, and lowering the jaw enlarges the mouth's resonant cavity. The oral cavity's overall effect on sound production can be demonstrated by humming a steady note while moving the lips, jaw, and tongue. The sounds coming out of the mouth vary even though the vocal folds continue to vibrate at the same frequency.

The *palate* plays a role in speech as well. Consisting of three parts, it forms the roof of the mouth. The palate's *alveolar ridge* is the shelf right behind the upper teeth. The tongue presses close to or against it to produce sounds such as \t\ and \s\. The *hard palate* is the firm, domed portion of the mouth's roof, and the *soft palate*, also known as the *velum*, is flexible tissue behind the hard palate. One part of the soft palate, called the *uvula*, hangs like a pendulum at the back of the mouth. It lifts to close the *velopharyngeal port*, an opening that connects the nasal cavities and pharynx, preventing some sounds from entering the *nasal cavity* (which consists of passageways behind the cheekbones and leading to the nostrils) and resonating there. The nasal cavity is, however, used to produce the nasal sounds of speech, such as the consonants in the word *mining*.

The sound that eventually leaves the mouth is a combination of the sound waves produced by the larynx and the resonant response of the vocal tract. Voice sound waves not only travel through the air but

Nineteenth-century researcher Johannes Müller developed a theory describing how air movement, muscle tension in the larynx, and the flexibility of the vocal cords combine to create audible puffs of air used in speech.

through the bones of the speaker's own skull as well. However, voice waves transmitted through the skull sound different to the speaker than they do to others, and that is why a tape recording of one's own voice often sounds odd.

STRESS AND INTONATION

During speech many of the sound patterns extend across syllables, words, or a whole sentence. These patterns, which can be in the form of stress on a single word or an intonation pattern throughout a sentence, add meaning to a person's speech. They can change the definition of words, denote questions, or express attitudes. The rhythm and tonal patterns of speech are called *prosody*.

Stress

By stressing a word or syllable a speaker usually increases the intensity, pitch, and duration of the stressed sound. Almost all words have a stressed syllable. The syllable that is stressed can distinguish the meaning of a word, often between its verb and noun forms. When the first syllable in the word *digest* is stressed, the word is a noun meaning a systematic arrangement of condensed data, as in the *Reader's Digest*. When the second syllable is stressed, however, the word becomes a verb meaning to transform food into a form that can be absorbed by the body. Stressing a word can also emphasize its importance in a sentence.

Intonation

The pitch of a person's voice rises and falls during a sentence. When intonation rises at the end, this often signals a question that can be answered either yes or no, as in "Did you *take it*?" Normal declarative sentences and questions that cannot be answered in yes-or-no form rise and then fall at the end. Speakers often pause during a sentence but raise the pitch of their voice just before the pause to signal that they plan to continue talking. Moreover, intonation can add meaning or express an attitude so strongly that the tonal meaning can override the meaning of the words. When a person uses a sarcastic tone of voice to say, "Oh, that's just great," most people know that the opposite is meant. Excitement is often signaled by widely varying intonations, while calmness or boredom are communicated through a relatively steady intonation.

CHAPTER FIVE

THE EAR

The ability to hear is essential to acquiring speech.

The human ear vibrates in response to sound waves, then converts those vibrations into nerve impulses that are sent to the brain for processing and interpretation. The human ear can sense sound waves between 20 and 20,000 Hz and is especially sensitive to waves common to human speech, which fall between 100 and 5,000 Hz. In effect, the human ear is tuned to the sounds humans produce.

The ear is divided into three parts—the *outer ear*, *middle ear*, and *inner ear*—each of which performs a different function. The outer ear funnels sound to the middle ear while amplifying some of the higher frequencies. It also protects the delicate middle ear from physical damage. The middle ear, containing the three smallest bones in the human body, converts the sound waves from air pressure fluctuations into mechanical vibrations and transmits those vibrations to the liquid of the inner ear. The inner ear separates complex sounds into their individual components, a series of simple sine waves. It then transforms that information into nerve impulses that travel to the brain. The inner ear also maintains the body's sense of balance and physical orientation in space.

OUTER EAR

The outer ear consists of the externally visible portion of the ear and the *auditory canal*, a one-inch air-filled cavity that ends at the *eardrum*. The portion of the ear that is visible from the outside is called the *pinna*, or *auricle*. It funnels sound into the auditory canal, performing slightly better on sounds that come from in front of the listener than from

The ear is divided into three parts; each section performs its own separate function in a process that converts sound waves into nerve impulses, which are then transmitted to the brain.

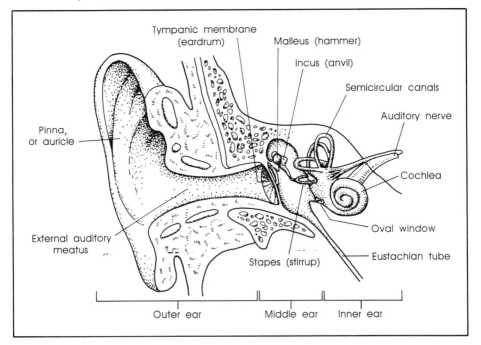

behind. In addition, it amplifies higher frequencies, which because of certain characteristics that low frequency waves do not have, are particularly important in helping the ears determine the location of a sound source. The pinna—particularly the small projection at the front of the auditory canal, called the *tragus*—also offers some physical protection for the rest of the ear.

The auditory canal, also known as the *auditory meatus*, protects the middle ear by keeping out foreign objects. Glands in the auditory canal secrete earwax, called *cerumen*, which, aided by hairs in the canal, filters out potentially damaging dust and flying insects. The canal also maintains a relatively constant inner temperature and humidity at the eardrum. In addition, it acts as a resonator, amplifying sounds between 3,000 and 4,000 Hz.

MIDDLE EAR

Sound waves traveling down the auditory canal strike the eardrum, a thin, semitransparent, oval-shaped membrane that is just a fraction of a square inch in size. The eardrum is so named because it resembles the skin stretched across a drum, although it is also known as the *tympanic membrane*. The eardrum vibrates in response to sound waves and is attached to the *malleus*, or *hammer*, the first of the middle ear's

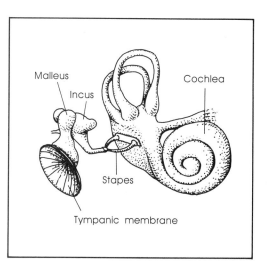

The middle ear is responsible for increasing the intensity of incoming sound waves and transforming them into mechanical vibrations that can easily travel through the inner ear.

Malleus

Incus

Cochlea

Stapes

Tympanic membrane

three bones. The eardrum's vibrations move the malleus, which in turn moves the *incus*, or *anvil*. The incus then moves the *stapes*, or *stirrup*, which is attached to the inner ear's membranous *oval window*.

The leverage of the middle ear bones increases the intensity of a sound wave by about 5 dB before the wave is funneled toward the oval window. Since the eardrum is almost 20 times larger than the oval window, the energy from the eardrum's vibration becomes more concentrated at the window, raising the sound wave's intensity an extra 25 decibels.

The middle ear also provides another crucial step between incoming sound waves and the inner ear. If the waves traveled directly from the outer ear to the oval window, which has liquid on its inner side, much of the sound would reflect back out of the ear. However, because the middle ear converts the sound waves into mechanical vibrations, the sound is efficiently transferred into the liquid. The middle ear conducts vibrations most efficiently in the 500- to 4,000-Hz range, key frequencies for speech.

Middle ear muscles, the smallest in the body, sometimes flex in response to sound waves above 85 dB, reducing the intensity of sound waves moving through the middle ear toward the inner ear. Scientists are not sure why this action, known as the *middle ear reflex*, or *acoustic reflex*, occurs. Some suggest that it may help prevent damage to the delicate structures of the inner ear, although the reflex is too slow to protect against sudden loud noises such as gunshots. The muscles do flex, however, just before a person speaks, prompting a theory that the acoustic reflex may offer protection against the intensity of one's own voice as it travels through the bones of the skull and into the ear.

The *eustachian tube*, an air-filled canal running from the middle ear to the back of the throat, assures that air pressure inside and outside the middle ear remains identical. If the two air pressures are different, the eardrum will not respond correctly to the pressure fluctuations in sound waves. Just about anyone who has flown in an airplane has felt this effect. As the plane rises sharply toward its cruising altitude, cabin pressure drops, so that air pressure inside a passenger's ears becomes

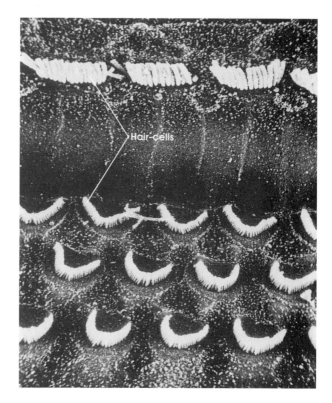

Located within the inner ear, the organ of Corti changes mechanical vibrations into electrical impulses. When the organ vibrates, special cells, known as hair cells, are disturbed, setting off the transmission of signals to the brain.

greater than it is outside. The ears feel uncomfortable, and sounds are muffled. Swallowing or yawning opens the eustachian tube, allowing the pressure to equalize and sound to again be conducted normally through the ears.

INNER EAR

The inner ear transforms vibrations in liquid into nerve impulses that are sent to the brain, a process carried out via the *cochlea, basilar membrane, organ of Corti*, and *auditory nerve*.

Cochlea and Basilar Membrane

The cochlea is a bony, snail-shaped organ filled with fluid. Within the cochlea, a chamber called the *cochlear partition* runs almost its entire length. The partition is bounded on one side by the basilar membrane and on the other by the *vestibular membrane*.

When sound enters the ear, the *footplate* of the stirrup-shaped stapes vibrates the oval window, producing vibrations within the fluid of the cochlea. This, in turn, disturbs the basilar membrane. Different parts of the membrane vibrate according to the frequency of the incoming waves. The *base*, the narrow and stiff end near the oval window, vibrates most when agitated by high-frequency waves. The *apex* is wider and more flexible and responds to lower-frequency sounds.

Organ of Corti

The organ of Corti sits on the basilar membrane inside the cochlear partition and performs the actual transformation of mechanical vibrations into nerve impulses. It has a gelatinous *tectorial membrane* and two sets of *hair cells*, inner and outer, sitting between the basilar and tectorial membranes. When the basilar membrane vibrates it pushes the hair cells against the tectorial membrane. That action causes the hair

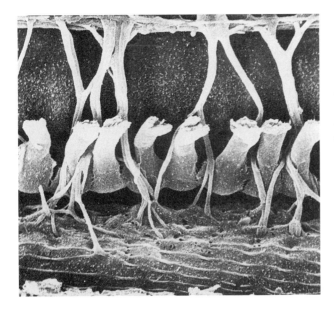

Tens of thousands of nerve fibers combine to form the auditory nerve. Chemicals secreted from the hair cells stimulate electrical impulses in these fibers. The signals are transmitted to the brain, which interprets them as sound.

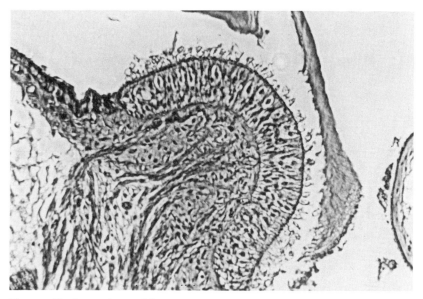

The vestibular system of the inner ear perceives movement and maintains balance.

cells to produce a special chemical that triggers electrical impulses in adjacent nerve fibers. These fibers, approximately 30,000 of them, transmit the signals to both the brain stem and the brain's *auditory cortex*. Reading these impulses, the brain can pinpoint the section of the basilar membrane that produced most of the signals and in this way determine the frequency of the incoming sound. The pattern of the signals also appears to deliver sound-related information, since some of the nerve cells fire at the same frequency as the sound wave stimulating them, and others fire more quickly as the sound becomes louder.

In addition, research suggests that the outer hair cells may actually help the basilar membrane tune into specific frequencies and pick up milder sounds. Experiments indicate, for example, that the hairs can lengthen or shorten in response to nerve messages coming from the brain. Scientists also suspect that when the basilar membrane is focused on a specific frequency, nerve fibers picking up other frequencies from the membrane transmit their messages less effectively, allowing the desired frequency to stand out.

The inner ear contains three semicircular coils and two small chambers that together make up the *vestibular system*. By perceiving movement and acceleration, this system allows humans to maintain balance and walk upright.

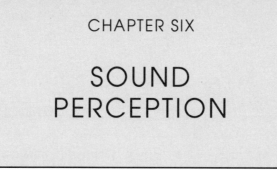

CHAPTER SIX

SOUND PERCEPTION

Ventriloquists, such as the late Edgar Bergen, have always relied on the eyes' ability to alter the brain's perception of sound. The human partner talks but the dummy's lips move, creating the illusion that the doll is speaking.

Once the brain receives neural impulses from the inner ear, it analyzes and decodes the information carried on the sound waves, registering data about the intensity, frequency, and source of the sound. In the special case of speech, the brain also deciphers the message included in the wave.

LOCALIZATION AND SEGREGATION

Having two ears allows humans to determine the direction from which a sound originates. Humans judge direction primarily by noting the difference in time and intensity between the sound waves reaching their two ears. A sound coming from the right will reach a person's right ear first, although the time difference can be as a small as a millisecond (one thousandth of a second). In addition, because the head is in the way of the sound wave, the left ear also will receive a slightly less intense sound in this case. Humans are not consciously aware of these time and intensity differences but unconsciously process them to produce a sense of direction. The outer portion of the ear also helps to determine the direction of a sound source. Sound waves bounce inside the folds of the pinna before entering the ear canal, slightly altering the frequency of the waves. The direction of the waves also has an effect on the angle at which they hit the pinna and, as a result, on how their frequency is changed. The brain can sense these differences and use them to determine the direction of the sound source. Sounds coming from directly in front of or behind a person will have no time or

Through the use of two ears, the direction of a sound source can be located based on both the difference in time it takes for sound waves to reach each ear and the variations in the sound's intensity from one ear to the other.

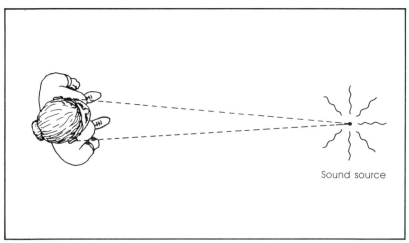

Sound source

intensity differences and can be confusing. When unsure about the source of a sound, people often turn their heads to create those differences and use them to localize the sound.

The eyes also help to localize sounds. Their message is so powerful, in fact, that they can help trick a listener. In movie theaters, for example, the speakers are usually positioned on either side of the auditorium, but because viewers see the actors moving their lips, the sound seems to come from the screen itself. In addition, a ventriloquist's dummy cannot speak, but because its lips move and the ventriloquist's do not, the puppet seems to be doing the talking. The ability of the eyes to override information from the ears can be valuable because auditory information is sometimes wrong. For example, an echo may come from one direction while the original source is somewhere else.

It would be much easier to sense loudness, pitch, and direction if sounds arrived one at a time. In most situations, however, humans never hear one sound wave by itself. Sound waves from several different sources commonly enter the ear at once, and none of them has a label saying this frequency is a lawn mower and that one a fan. Why is it, then, that sounds do not form an auditory goulash in which none of the individual components are distinguishable? It is because the human brain is adept at finding relationships and patterns within complex stimuli. All the frequency components from one source tend to start, stop, rise, and fall together. These components are then grouped into a conceptual whole and perceived as a single sound.

Not only can a person distinguish between several different sounds at once, he or she can selectively focus on one at a time, such as picking out one voice in a room full of chattering people. Researchers do not know exactly how humans do this, but it appears to result from having two ears and the ability to determine the direction of a sound source. In one experiment, for example, researchers placed a set of headphones on a test subject and played two sounds in one ear: a pure tone and the scratchy noise of static. Then the scientists increased the static noise until it drowned out the pure tone. Interestingly enough, however, when the researchers then began to play the static noise alone in the subject's other ear, the first ear, which was still receiving both sounds, was suddenly able to hear the pure tone again above the static. Apparently, when the static and pure tone are simultaneously presented to, for example, the left ear, the fact that both are coming from the same direction makes them indistinguishable. When static is played in the right ear, however, it fools the listener into thinking the static and pure tone in the left ear are each coming from a different direction, and when that happens, both sounds can be heard separately.

FEEDBACK

Scientists have learned that a speaker listens to his or her own voice in order to ascertain whether the message is being sent correctly. This phenomenon, called *auditory feedback*, was discovered accidentally in 1950 by a New Jersey engineer named Bernard Lee. While recording himself he found that if he wore headphones and heard the sound of his voice a fraction of a second after he spoke, he became unable to talk properly; he repeated some syllables and overly prolonged others. People will adjust their speech depending upon what they hear themselves say. When Lee heard his words slightly after he spoke them instead of simultaneously, his brain mistakenly registered the idea that pronunciation errors were being made and tried to correct the perceived problem. The delay in time, however, caused even further mistakes to be made.

With the use of two ears, humans can focus on a single voice in a crowded playground or a noisy room.

SPEECH PERCEPTION

Understanding speech requires the most complex type of sound perception humans are capable of because they must deal with sounds coming in rapid succession and that vary from one speaker to another. For example, a child speaks at a higher frequency than an adult does, and a Southern drawl is far different than an East Coast accent. Nonetheless, humans use a variety of acoustic cues in the sound wave to distinguish phonemes, syllables, and words. However, nonacoustic cues are also vital to efficient communication. What a person sees and already knows about a specific situation can help when the acoustic cues are ambiguous.

That humans can understand and extract meaning from speech is extraordinary considering the speed, complexity, and variability of its sound waves. Humans transmit and interpret speech information more rapidly than they can absorb other kinds of information. If, for example, a person taps a pencil against a hard surface faster than seven to nine times per second, the individual taps become indistinguishable. At about 15 taps per second, a person hears only a buzz. Yet during speech people frequently produce anywhere from 20 to 30 phonemes per second.

To make matters even more complicated, people speak so rapidly that sounds overlap and mix, a phenomenon called *coarticulation.* Researchers at Haskins Laboratories, currently located in New Haven, Connecticut, discovered coarticulation in the late 1940s while trying to develop a machine that could read aloud to blind people. The scientists thought that if they got a sample of all 47 English speech sounds, the machine could just combine them to produce all the words in the English language. The researchers recorded people saying a variety of words, then tried to cut the tape into small sections that would isolate the individual sounds. With the word *cat*, for example, they tried to cut the magnetic tape into its individual phonemes \k\, \æ\, and \t\. They failed, however, finding that no matter how they cut the tape the \k\ always included portions of the \æ\. The \æ\ either had parts of the \k\ or parts of the \t\. Moreover, when the researchers tried to

The Voder (Voice Operation Demonstrator) was invented in the 1930s by electrical engineer Homer Dudley, who used various frequencies and intensities to electronically synthesize the sounds of speech.

reassemble these imperfectly separated sounds into other words the results were largely unintelligible.

Speech Perception Theories

There is little agreement on just how people extract meaning from the sound waves of speech, but most researchers support either *active* or *passive* theories of perception.

Proponents of active theories believe that the brain takes an active role in decoding speech sounds. One of the leading versions of this idea was proposed by Alvin Liberman and his colleagues. Their *motor theory* suggests that people refer to the way they themselves produce speech sounds in order to understand what others are saying, even though each person may not pronounce the same word in the exact same way. These researchers also believe that people go into a speech mode of perception that is different from the way they listen to other sounds. There is evidence that the human brain contains special neural circuits for this purpose.

Proponents of passive theories believe that speech perception is primarily a sensory activity. They suggest that, despite their variability, all speech sounds have certain characteristics that remain the same. When someone is talking, a listener can recognize the features of speech that do not vary and use them to interpret what the speaker is saying, despite a foreign accent or some other wrinkle that makes one voice sound different from another.

Technological advances over the past 60 years have played a vital role in understanding speech perception. In the 1930s, Homer Dudley, an electrical engineer at Bell Telephone Laboratories (now AT&T Bell Laboratories), created an electronic speech synthesizer called the Voice Operation Demonstrator, or Voder. Previous attempts at speech synthesis had failed after researchers tried to copy the physical features and movements of the vocal tract. The Voder, however, used acoustic features, including various frequencies and intensities, to produce sounds that—although they would never be confused with a human voice—could still be recognized as speech. Continuing this emphasis on acoustic features, Ralph Potter, also at Bell Labs, developed a machine called a *sound spectrograph*. This device analyzes and graphs the changing frequencies of speech. The graph is known as a *sound spectrogram*.

Both the Voder and the sound spectrograph helped researchers determine the features of sound waves people use to comprehend the spoken word. The scientists learned that although the fundamental

The sound spectrograph, invented by Ralph Potter, analyzes changes in the frequencies of speech and reproduces these changes graphically either on paper or on a computer screen.

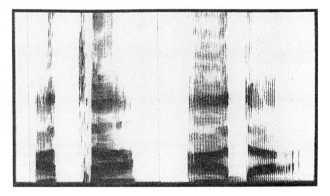

frequency of a particular tone determines pitch, it has little to do with whether or not a word is actually intelligible. Instead, listeners use the harmonics of a tone to distinguish speech sounds. Intensity and timing of the sounds also play a role.

Commonsense Clues

Regardless of whether the active or passive theories of speech perception hold true, however, these are not the only methods used to decipher what is being said. As one researcher put it, they simply offer "a rough guide to the sense of the message, a kind of scaffolding upon which the listener constructs or reconstructs sentences." Depending upon who is speaking, what he or she is talking about, and the other words in the sentence, a listener can guess what some words will be. This means that to some extent, people hear what they expect to hear.

One researcher substituted a cough for a word and found that instead of noticing the cough, the listener thought that he had heard the missing word. People also watch lips and facial expressions to help them decipher speech. So many different cues are used to decipher speech that even under difficult circumstances—when there is a loud background noise, for example—people will often find enough cues to understand what is being said. This makes speech a very reliable mode of communication.

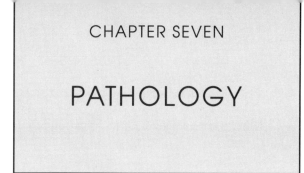

CHAPTER SEVEN

PATHOLOGY

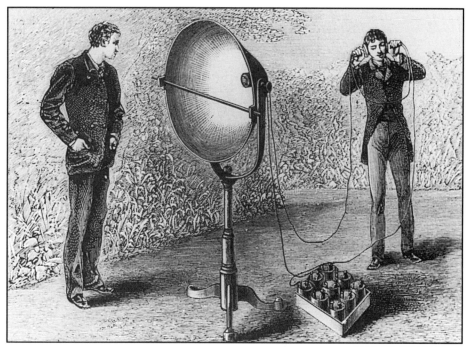

This early hearing aid was developed by Alexander Graham Bell, teacher of the deaf and inventor of the telephone.

Effective communication depends on what researchers Peter Denes and Elliott Pinson called the *speech chain*. This includes the speaker's brain and vocal tract; the medium, such as air, through which the sound waves travel; and the listener's ear and brain. If any of the links in the chain weaken or break, communication can be disrupted. The result may be a speech, hearing, or language disorder.

DIAGNOSING LANGUAGE DISORDERS

To determine whether someone has a communication problem, a specialist can examine abilities in five different areas:

1. *Phonology*, which deals with the patient's comprehension of speech sounds.

2. *Semantics*, which refers to the ability to understand the meaning of words.

3. *Syntax*, which applies to how well a person is able to place words in the correct order.

4. *Morphology*, which deals with the ability to use prefixes and suffixes.

5. *Pragmatics*, which refers to the proper use of language in social situations; that is, how well the patient is able to initiate conversation, take turns speaking, and use the proper language when addressing different people (e.g., does a child speak differently to a teacher than he or she does to other youngsters?).

Many communication disorders can be effectively treated through therapy or medical intervention, and some can be compensated for with artificial speech and hearing devices. Generally, however, the earlier a problem is diagnosed the more effective treatment will be.

SPEECH DISORDERS

Everyone misspeaks at one time or another, by pausing or repeating a word or part of a word. In fact, most children, usually at about two and a half to three and a half years old, go through a brief period of *disfluency*, when their speech is not fluid or fluent. This happens when they are trying to graduate from one- and two-word utterances to more complex sentences. Sometimes, however, disfluency can be a long-lasting and serious problem.

Stuttering

Approximately 1% of the population—boys more often than girls—at some point in life begin to stutter. About 85% of those who do, start while still preschoolers, and close to 80% recover without any help. If the impediment does not correct itself, however, stuttering can become a very serious problem because it stops the flow of communication.

A person who stutters usually does it in one or more of three specific ways. These include repeating words or sounds (ta-ta-ta-ta-ta-ble), prolonging sounds abnormally (ssssssssilence), or failing to emit sound from the vocal folds. People who stutter also often display secondary behaviors such as head jerking, eye blinking, and facial grimaces, all of which appear to be associated with the extraordinary effort being made to speak. Although it is tempting to help a person making such an effort, most stutterers say that they hate to have people finish words for them, preferring to complete what they are saying even if it takes some time.

Along with the communication difficulties it presents, stuttering can also cause feelings of both embarrassment and helplessness and can limit a person's confidence and self-esteem. As a result, a stutterer may avoid speaking on the telephone or might even answer questions incorrectly, just to avoid tackling a difficult word.

There are a host of theories concerning the causes behind stuttering. Because the disorder seems to run in families, some believe it could be a genetic disorder, although this has not been proved. A more widely

Therapists can employ a variety of methods to cure speech disorders. The earlier a problem is diagnosed, however, the more effective treatment is likely to be.

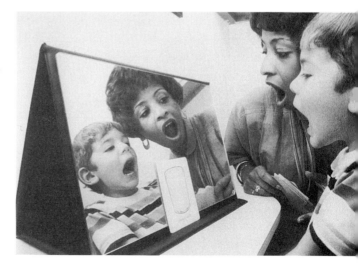

accepted theory suggests that some parents become overly concerned when they notice their youngster going through a period of normal childhood disfluency. As a result, the adults inadvertently create an atmosphere of tension and anxiety in the household that actually causes the child to continue stuttering.

There are numerous other theories that attribute the cause to neuroses, conditioning, biochemical, or physiological factors, but as of now, no one knows for certain what causes a person to stutter, and no consistently effective therapies have been developed. Generally, however, speech-language pathologists are more successful at treating a young person who is just beginning to stutter than at helping an adolescent or adult who has stuttered for a long time. Therapists often attempt to cure stuttering by working to reduce the anxiety a patient associates with the disorder, either by changing the patient's environment, teaching the stutterer to feel less stressed, or changing the way parents interact with children who stutter.

Articulation Disorders

Articulation is the precise movement of the tongue, lips, and jaw in the production of speech. When people, most often young children, fail to move the parts of the vocal tract accurately enough to make themselves understood, they are said to have an articulation problem. The most common communication disorder among school-age children, articulation trouble accounts for approximately 80% of an elementary school speech-language pathologist's caseload.

Children with articulation problems make at least one of four kinds of errors. Sometimes they substitute one sound for another that is easier to say. They might, for example, substitute \w\ for \r\ and say "wabbit" instead of "rabbit." They may omit sounds, perhaps saying, "My ca is gone" when they mean to say either "My cat is gone" or "My cap is gone." They might also distort some sounds, although words may still be recognizable. In rare cases the child will add a sound, saying, for example, "buhlack" instead of "black."

The cause behind an articulation disorder is generally considered to be either *organic* or *functional*. An organic cause is a physical or neurological problem, such as a cleft palate (in which the palate fails to completely close during the development of the fetus), cerebral palsy, or even a hearing loss that prevents the youngster from hearing and imitating sounds. In other cases, according to one theory, children do not notice the differences between sounds and thus do not imitate them accurately. Another theory suggests that some youngsters fail to develop the motor skills needed to produce the proper speech sounds. In most cases, however, the condition has no proven cause.

Nevertheless, several therapeutic strategies have been effective in treating articulation problems. Sometimes children are taught to discriminate between the correct and incorrect way to pronounce sounds. On other occasions, a speech-language pathologist uses a behavioral approach, responding to the child's statements when the youngster speaks correctly but not when the child mispronounces words.

Voice Disorders

Problems with the pitch, loudness, or quality of a person's speech are called *voice disorders*. They can result from a physical deformity, such as a cleft palate, or from abnormal growths that prevent the folds from vibrating properly. For example, a singer who performs too often may end up with nodes on his or her folds that must be surgically removed. In extreme cases, such as cancer, a patient might have to have a diseased or damaged larynx taken out.

HEARING IMPAIRMENT

Hearing impairment is the most common communication disorder, affecting people in all age groups. Among childhood ailments, for example, only the common cold occurs more frequently than *otitis media*, an inflammation of the middle ear. *Presbycusis*, a form of hearing impairment associated with aging, affects as many as 27 million Americans over age 65. Hearing impairment is usually divided into two categories, *conductive* and *sensorineural*. Hearing aids can be helpful, especially for patients with conductive hearing loss.

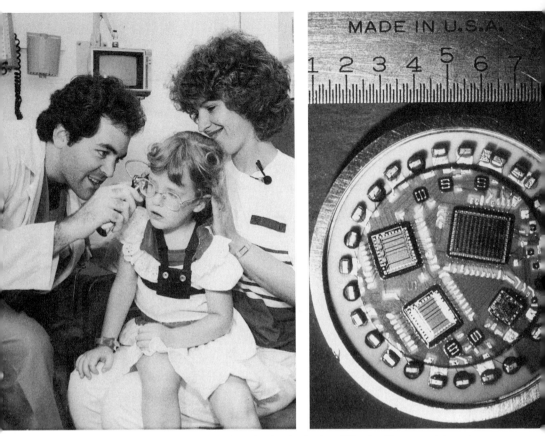

This child is being examined prior to being fitted with a cochlear implant. The implant (right) is designed to replace damaged hair cells, allowing electrical sound impulses to be transmitted to the brain.

Conductive Hearing Impairment

Conductive problems result when sound waves cannot travel properly through the outer and middle ear. Otitis media is one example of this type of impairment. The condition, which can be quite painful, results when inflammation causes fluid and pressure to build up in the inner ear. If untreated, it can cause permanent hearing loss. Another conductive hearing problem, *otosclerosis*, is caused by a hardening of the middle ear bones and afflicts some older people. Conductive hearing loss can also result from a torn eardrum (which can be caused by an extremely loud noise, such as the bang of a gunshot next to the ear). In some cases the damaged eardrum can be surgically repaired. When conductive hearing loss occurs, the ability to hear all sound frequencies is equally impaired.

Sensorineural Hearing Impairment

Sensorineural hearing impairment occurs in the inner ear and usually involves irreparable damage to the hair cells. Unlike conductive hearing loss, however, it tends to affect some frequencies more than others. As a result, people suffering from this condition frequently say that they can hear people speak but cannot understand what is being said. Hearing aids are less helpful for people with sensorineural loss than for those with conductive problems.

Prolonged exposure to loud sounds from heavy machinery, stereo headphones, or rock music concerts is a common cause of sensorineural hearing loss. Noise exceeding 80 dB is considered potentially hazardous, and the louder the noise, the less exposure is required before damage occurs. If a person has to raise his or her voice to be heard over surrounding noise, it may indicate that the sound level is potentially damaging. If speech sounds muffled or dull after leaving a noisy area, then the volume was definitely too high. Ringing or pain in the ears also indicates dangerously loud noise.

LANGUAGE DISORDERS

Language problems are more complex and less recognizable than speech or hearing difficulties. Language disorders involve the inability to choose words and form sentences and can be part of more general problems. Moreover, they can be divided into two categories: *developmental* and *acquired.*

Developmental Language Problems

Children who fail to develop a complete set of language skills have a developmental language problem. The causes are still unknown, but in many cases the disorder is only part of a broader problem that can include autism or mental retardation. Nonetheless, developmental difficulties can strike otherwise normal children as well.

Youngsters suffering from semantic difficulties find words with multiple meanings especially difficult. Those with syntax problems often put words in the wrong order, especially when trying to handle complex sentence constructions. Morphological difficulties are recognizable in children who ignore word endings. Youngsters with pragmatics problems not only use a simpler style of communication than do their peers but also tend not to use polite terms or show consideration for their listeners. Any of these disorders can raise a child's risk of academic failure, even if he or she is intelligent enough to succeed. Speech-language therapy can help children suffering from a developmental problem, although many will face a measure of difficulty throughout life.

Cross section of a stroke victim's brain. A massive hemorrhage caused the right hemisphere to enlarge.

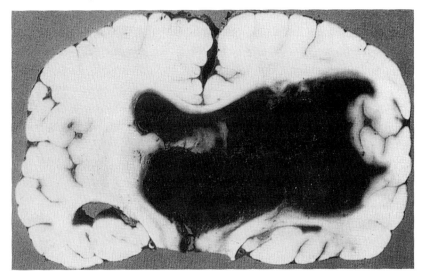

Acquired Language Problems

Aphasia is the most common form of acquired language disability and results in difficulty expressing and comprehending linguistic symbols. The condition is usually caused by a stroke but can result from other problems as well, such as *encephalitis* (swelling of the brain) or a head injury. The damage usually occurs in the left hemisphere of the cerebral cortex, which is where both Broca's and Wernicke's areas are located.

Aphasia is divided into *fluent* and *nonfluent* categories. Fluent aphasia is most often associated with the rear portion of the left hemisphere, in and around Wernicke's area. Nonfluent aphasia usually results from damage located farther toward the front of the hemisphere, in or near Broca's area.

The fluent form of the disorder includes Wernicke's aphasia (see Chapter Two) and *anomic aphasia*, in which the patient has difficulty retrieving the precise word that he or she wants to say. As a result, the sufferer tends to replace the lost word with a substitute, such as "thing" or "this." People with *conduction aphasia*, on the other hand, often use inappropriate sounds or words, even though they have good language comprehension. Broca's aphasia (see Chapter Two) is the most common form of the nonfluent disorder.

Although aphasia can result in serious communication problems, the patient may recover naturally over a period of months. Therapy can also be helpful. Full recovery, however, is more likely for children than for adults. Researchers believe that the opposite side of the brain, as well as tissue adjacent to Broca's and Wernicke's areas, sometimes assume functions previously controlled by the damaged areas.

This suggests that human beings possess a communication system that is not only remarkably complex but resilient as well. Certainly other animals may be blessed with enviable qualities: tremendous strength, sensitive smell, impressive vision, or unmatched speed. Yet it is the human ability to communicate—to speak in any number of languages, to investigate the soul through the words of William Shakespeare, or to sit with the representatives of many nations and argue with words instead of weapons—that makes spoken language a very special gift indeed.

APPENDIX:
FOR MORE INFORMATION

The following is a list of national organizations and associations in the United States and Canada that can provide further information about speech, language, and hearing disorders.

GENERAL INFORMATION

American Speech-Language-Hearing
    Association
10801 Rockville Pike
Rockville, MD 20852
(301) 897-5700
(800) 638-6868

Speech Foundation of America
P.O. Box 11749
Memphis, TN 38111
(901) 452-7343
(800) 992-9392

CLEFT PALATE

American Cleft Palate Association
1218 Grandview Avenue
Pittsburgh, PA 15211
(412) 481-1376
(800) 242-5338

Canadian Cleft Lip and Palate Family
    Association
180 Dundas Street West
Suite 1508
Toronto, Ontario
M5G 1X8
(416) 598-2311

DEAFNESS AND HEARING IMPAIRMENT

Alexander Graham Bell Association
    for the Deaf
3417 Volta Place NW
Washington, DC 20007
(202) 337-5220

American Hearing Research
    Foundation
55 East Washington Street
Suite 2022
Chicago, IL 60602
(312) 726-9670

Canadian Hearing Society
271 Spadina Road
Toronto, Ontario
M5R 2V3
(416) 964-9595 (voice)
(416) 964-0023 (telephone device for
    the deaf)

Hear Center
301 E. Del Mar Blvd.
Pasadena, CA 91101
(213) 681-4641

International Foundation for
   Children's Hearing Education
   and Research
928 McLean Avenue
Yonkers, NY 10704
(914) 237-2676

Vancouver League for the Hard of
   Hearing
2125 West 7th Avenue
Vancouver, British Columbia
V6K 1X9
(604) 731-8010

HEARING AIDS

National Hearing Aid Society
20361 Middlebelt Road
Livonia, MI 48152
(313) 478-2610
(800) 521-5247

STUTTERING

National Stuttering Project
4601 Irving Street
San Francisco, CA 94122
(415) 566-5324

TINNITUS

American Tinnitus Association
P.O. Box 5
Portland, OR 97207
(503) 248-9985

Tinnitus Association of Canada
23 Ellis Park Road
Toronto, Ontario
M6S 2V4
(416) 762-1490

STATE LISTINGS

The following is a list of rehabilitation
programs in the United States that are
accredited by the Professional Services Board of the American Speech-
Language-Hearing Association in either
audiology or speech-language pathology and audiology.

ALABAMA

Speech and Hearing Center
University of South Alabama
Humanities Bldg., Room 40
Mobile, AL 36688
(205) 460-6327

Speech and Hearing Clinic
University of Alabama at Birmingham
UAB Station Box 503
University Station
Birmingham, AL 35294
(205) 934-4467

ALASKA

Communicative Disorders Program
Alaska Department of Health and Social
   Services
Gambel Street
Anchorage, AK 99501
(907) 562-2675

ARIZONA

Audiology Department
Good Samaritan Medical Center
1111 E. McDowell Road
Phoenix, AZ 85006
(602) 239-4577

ARKANSAS

Children's Hearing and Speech Clinic
Arkansas Department of Health
4815 W. Markham Street
Little Rock, AR 72201
(501) 661-2328

CALIFORNIA

Audiology and Speech Clinic
School of Medicine
University of California, Los Angeles
10833 LeConte Avenue
Los Angeles, CA 90024
(213) 825-8551

Communications Clinic
Department of Communicative
    Disorders
San Diego State University
5300 Campanile Drive
San Diego, CA 92182
(619) 594-6477

Providence Speech and Hearing Center
1301 Providence Avenue
Orange, CA 92668
(714) 639-4990

San Francisco Hearing and Speech
    Center
1234 Divisadero Street
San Francisco, CA 94115
(415) 921-7658

COLORADO

Audiology and Speech Pathology
    Department
Children's Hospital
1056 E. 19th Avenue
Denver, CO 80218
(303) 861-6800

Speech/Language Pathology and
    Audiology Clinics
Department of Communication
    Disorders
University of Northern Colorado
Greeley, CO 80639
(303) 351-2012

CONNECTICUT

Southeastern Connecticut Hearing and
    Speech Center
92 New London Tpke.
Norwich, CT 06360
(203) 887-1654

DELAWARE

Hearing Center
Riverside Hospital
700 Lea Blvd.
Wilmington, DE 19899
(302) 764-6120

DISTRICT OF COLUMBIA

Speech and Hearing Center
2201 G Street NW
Room 407
Washington, DC 20052
(202) 994-7360

FLORIDA

Speech, Hearing, and Learning Services
Morton F. Plant Hospital
430 Pirellas Street
Clearwater, FL 33516
(813) 462-7031

Speech and Hearing Center
1128 Laura Street
Jacksonville, FL 32206
(904) 355-3403

GEORGIA

Atlanta Speech School
3160 Northside Pkwy. NW
Atlanta, GA 30327
(404) 233-5332

HAWAII

Audiology and Speech Pathology Clinic
Tripler Army Medical Center
Honolulu, HI 96859
(808) 433-5719

ILLINOIS

Communication Disorders Department
Jayne Shover Easter Seal Rehabilitation
    Center
799 South McLean Blvd.
Elgin, IL 60120
(708) 742-3264

Department of Communicative
    Disorders
Rehabilitation Institute of Chicago
345 E. Superior Street
Chicago, IL 60611
(312) 908-6138

INDIANA

Speech and Hearing Center
Indiana University
Bloomington, IN 47405
(812) 855-6251

Speech Pathology and Audiology
    Department
Crossroads Rehabilitation Center
4740 Kingsway Drive
Indianapolis, IN 46025
(317) 466-1000

IOWA

Des Moines Hearing and Speech Center
3004 30th Street
Des Moines, IA 50310
(515) 279-9034

KANSAS

Institute of Logopedics
2400 Jardine Drive
Wichita, KS 67219
(316) 262-8271

KENTUCKY

Hearing and Speech Center
Kentucky Easter Seal Society
233 E. Broadway
Louisville, KY 40202
(502) 584-9781

LOUISIANA

New Orleans Speech and Hearing
    Center
1636 Toledano Street
New Orleans, LA 70115
(504) 897-2606

Speech, Language, and Audiology
    Department
200 Henry Clay Avenue
New Orleans, LA 70118
(504) 899-9511

MAINE

Northeast Hearing and Speech Center
43 Baxter Blvd.
Portland, ME 04101
(207) 874-1065

MARYLAND

Division of Speech, Language, &
    Hearing
Baltimore County Department of Health
Eastern Regional Health Center
9100 Franklin Square Drive
Baltimore, MD 21237
(301) 687-6500

MASSACHUSETTS

Audiology Department
Massachusetts Eye and Ear Infirmary
243 Charles Street
Boston, MA 02114
(617) 523-7900

MICHIGAN

Speech/Language Pathology and
    Audiology Section
Department of Rehabilitation Medicine
Sinai Hospital of Detroit
6767 W. Outer Drive
Detroit, MI 48235
(313) 493-6315

Speech and Hearing Department
McLaren General Hospital
401 Ballenger Hwy.
Flint, MI 48532-3685
(313) 762-2362

MISSISSIPPI

Speech and Hearing Clinic
Mississippi University for Women
P.O. Box W-1340
Columbus, MS 39701
(601) 329-7270

MISSOURI

Hearing, Language, and Speech Clinic
Central Institute for the Deaf
818 South Euclid Street
St. Louis, MO 63110
(314) 652-3200

Hearing and Speech Departments
Children's Mercy Hospital
24th and Gillham Road
Kansas City, MO 64108
(816) 234-3677

MONTANA

Human Development Center
University of Montana
Missoula, MT 59812
(406) 243-4131

NEBRASKA

Clinical Communication Sciences
    Division
Boys Town Institute for Communication
    Disorders in Children
555 N. 30th Street
Omaha, NE 68131
(402) 498-6511

Speech and Hearing Clinic
Department of Special Education and
    Communication Disorders
University of Nebraska, Lincoln
253-A Barkley Memorial Center
Lincoln, NE 68583-0731
(402) 472-2071

NEW JERSEY

Speech and Hearing Department
Robert Wood Johnson, Jr. Rehabilitation
    Institute
65 James Street
Edison, NJ 08817-3059
(201) 321-7063

NEW MEXICO

Audiology Section
Lovelace Medical Center
5400 Gibson Blvd. SE
Albuquerque, NM 87108
(505) 262-7261

NEW YORK

Hearing and Speech Center of Rochester
1000 Elmwood Avenue

Rochester, NY 14620
(716) 271-0680

Speech and Hearing Division
Beth Israel Medical Center
First Avenue at East 16th Street
New York, NY 10003
(212) 420-2760

NORTH CAROLINA

Charlotte Speech and Hearing Center
300 South Caldwell Street
Charlotte, NC 28202
(704) 376-1342

Southeastern Speech and Hearing Services of North Carolina
226 Bradford Avenue
P.O. Box 53415
Fayetteville, NC 28305
(919) 485-5145

NORTH DAKOTA

Department of Communication
Disorders
Medical Center Rehabilitation Hospital
1300 South Columbia Road
Grand Forks, ND 58201
(701) 780-2447

OHIO

Cincinnati Speech and Hearing Center
3021 Vernon Place
Cincinnati, OH 45701
(513) 221-0527

Cleveland Hearing and Speech Center
11206 Euclid Avenue
Cleveland, OH 44106
(216) 231-8787

OKLAHOMA

Speech and Hearing Clinic

University of Oklahoma Health
Sciences Center
825 NE 14th Street
Oklahoma City, OK 73104
(405) 271-4214

OREGON

Eugene Hearing and Speech Center
1202 Almaden Street
Box 2087
Eugene, OR 97402
(503) 485-8521

Portland Center for Hearing and Speech
3515 SW Veterans Hospital Road
Portland, OR 97201
(503) 228-6479

PENNSYLVANIA

Center for Communication Disorders
12th Street and Taber Road
Philadelphia, PA 19141
(215) 329-5715

Pittsburgh Hearing, Speech, and Deaf
Services
1945 Fifth Avenue
Pittsburgh, PA 15219
(412) 232-7773

RHODE ISLAND

Hearing and Speech Center
Rhode Island Hospital
593 Eddy Street
Providence, RI 02902
(401) 277-5485

SOUTH CAROLINA

Pee Dee Speech and Hearing Center
153 N. Baroody Street
P.O. Box 804

Florence, SC 29503
(803) 662-7802

Speech and Hearing Clinic
University of South Carolina
1601 Street Julian Place
Columbia, SC 29204
(803) 777-2614

TENNESSEE

Speech and Hearing Center
Memphis State University
807 Jefferson Avenue
Memphis, TN 38105
(901) 678-5800

TEXAS

Callier Center for Communication
    Disorders
University of Texas at Dallas
1966 Inwood Road
Dallas, TX 75235
(214) 905-3000

Speech and Hearing Center of El Paso
El Paso Medical Center
1501 Arizona, Suite 1-D
El Paso, TX 79902
(915) 533-2266

Speech and Hearing Institute
University of Texas Health Science
    Center at Houston
1343 Moursund Street
Houston, TX 77030
(713) 792-4500

UTAH

Bureau of Communicative Disorders
Utah Department of Health
44 Medical Drive
Salt Lake City, 84113
(801) 533-6175

VERMONT

Eleanor M. Luse Center for Com-
    munication Disorders
University of Vermont
Burlington, VT 05405
(802) 656-3861

VIRGINIA

Speech and Hearing Center
James Madison University
Harrisonburg, VA 22807
(703) 568-6491

Speech and Hearing Center
University of Virginia
109 Cabell Hall
Charlottesville, VA 29903
(804) 924-7107

WASHINGTON

Hearing, Speech, and Deafness Center
1620 18th Avenue
Seattle, WA 98122
(206) 323-5770

Speech and Hearing Clinic
University of Washington
4131 15th Avenue NE, JH-40
Seattle, WA 98195
(206) 543-5440

WISCONSIN

Department of Speech
    Pathology/Audiology
Marshfield Clinic
1000 N. Oak
Marshfield, WI 54449
(715) 387-5371

FURTHER READING

GENERAL INFORMATION

Aitchison, Jean. *The Articulate Mammal: An Introduction to Psycholinguistics.* 3rd ed. New York: Universe Books, 1989.

Berg, Richard E., and David G. Stork. *The Physics of Sound.* Englewood Cliffs, NJ: Prentice-Hall, 1982.

Borden, Gloria J., and Katherine S. Porter. *Speech Science Primer: Physiology, Acoustics and Perception of Speech.* 2nd ed. Baltimore: Williams and Wilkins, 1984.

Daniloff, R., et al. *The Physiology of Speech and Hearing: An Introduction.* Englewood Cliffs, NJ: Prentice-Hall, 1980.

Denes, Peter B., and Elliot N. Pinson. *The Speech Chain: The Physics and Biology of Spoken Language.* New York: Anchor Books, 1973.

Geschwind, Norman. "Specializations of the Human Brain." *Scientific American* (September 1979): 180 – 82.

Hockett, Charles F. "The Origin of Speech." *Scientific American* (September 1960): 88 – 96.

Horgan, John. "Free Radical: A Word (or Two) about Linguist Noam Chomsky." *Scientific American* (May 1990): 40 – 44.

Hudspeth, A. J. "How the Ear's Works Work." *Nature* 341 (October 1989): 397–404.

Liberman, Alvin M., and Ignatius G. Mattingly. "A Specialization for Speech Perception." *Science* 243 (January 1989): 489–94.

Lieberman, Philip. *The Biology and Evolution of Language.* Cambridge: Harvard University Press, 1984.

Lieberman, Philip, and Sheila E. Blumstein. *Speech Physiology, Speech Perception, and Acoustic Phonetics.* New York: Cambridge University Press, 1988.

Moore, Brian C. *An Introduction to the Psychology of Hearing.* 3rd ed. San Diego: Academic Press, 1989.

Motley, Michael T. "Slips of the Tongue." *Scientific American* 253 (September 1985): 116–18.

Oyer, Herbert J., et al. *Speech, Language, and Hearing Disorders: A Guide for the Teacher.* Boston: Little, Brown, 1986.

Sekuler, Robert, and Randolph Blake. *Perception.* 2nd ed. New York: McGraw-Hill, 1990.

DEAFNESS

Beagley, H. A. *Deafness: The Facts.* New York: Oxford University Press, 1984.

Calvert, Donald R., and Richard Silverman. *Speech and Deafness.* Rev. ed. Washington, DC: Alexander Graham Bell Association for the Deaf, 1983.

Harrison, Robert V. *The Biology of Hearing and Deafness.* Springfield, IL: Thomas, 1988.

Lutterman, David M. *Deafness in Perspective.* Boston: College-Hill, 1986.

Nash, Jeffrey E., and Anedith Nash. *Deafness in Society.* Lexington, MA: Lexington Books, 1981.

HEARING DISORDERS

Gerber, Sanford E., and George T. Mencher, eds. *Early Diagnosis of Hearing Loss.* Orlando, FL: Grune, 1978.

Helleberg, Marilyn M. *Your Hearing Loss: How to Break the Sound Barrier.* Chicago: Nelson Hall, 1979.

Meyerhoff, William L. *Disorders of Hearing.* Austin, TX: PRO-ED, 1986.

National Research Council. *Tinnitus: Facts, Theories and Treatments.* Washington, DC: National Academy Press, 1983.

SIGN LANGUAGE

Angelback, William A. *Yes, You Can Sign! American Sign Language Phrase Book.* Watkins Glen, NY: Century Publishers, N. d.

Kyle, Jim G., and Bencie Wolls, eds. *Deaf People and Their Language.* New York: Cambridge University Press, 1988.

————. *Language in Sign: An International Perspective on Sign Language.* New York: Routledge, Chapman and Hall, 1983.

SPEECH DISORDERS

Agranowitz, Aleen, and Milfed R. McKeown. *Aphasia Handbook: For Adults and Children.* Springfield, IL: Thomas, 1975.

Bloodstein, Oliver. *Speech Pathology: An Introduction.* 2nd ed. Boston: Houghton Mifflin, 1983.

Powers, Gene R. *Cleft Palate.* Austin, TX: PRO-ED, 1982.

Shames, George H., and Elizabeth Wiig, eds. *Human Communication Disorders: An Introduction.* 2nd ed. Columbus, OH: Merrill, 1987.

GLOSSARY

acoustic reflex middle ear reflex; middle ear muscles flex either before a person speaks or in response to sound waves above 85 decibels

acoustic resonator an enclosed body of air; an air-filled structure designed to vibrate at a particular frequency

acoustics the science that deals with production, control, transmission, reception, and effects of sound

acquired language problems problems in which a person has difficulty expressing and comprehending linguistic symbols usually as a result of damage to the left hemisphere of the brain

active theory of speech perception theory putting forth that the brain actively decodes speech sounds

amplitude feature of a sound wave; the pressure differences created by a vibrating object

anomic aphasia the acquired language problem in which the patient has difficulty retrieving words and replaces them with substitutes such as "thing" or "this"

aperiodic sound noise; sound produced by an object vibrating in no apparent pattern; does not contain tones

articulation disorder the disorder that occurs when a speaker fails to move the parts of his or her vocal tract accurately enough to be understood

arytenoid cartilages the two pyramid-shaped cartilages that sit at the back of the larynx and to which the vocal folds attach

assemblage errors errors that occur when a speaker has selected all the right sounds but misplaces words or parts of words within a sentence; suggests that people plan an entire phrase before saying it

auditory meatus auditory canal; a one-inch, air-filled cavity that begins in the outer ear and ends at the eardrum; carries sound to the middle ear and protects the middle ear from foreign objects

auditory nerve the nerve that transmits electrical impulses from the inner ear to the brain stem and the auditory cortex of the brain

basilar membrane the membrane that runs through the cochlea; vibrates in different parts depending on frequency of incoming sound waves and agitates the hair cells of the organ of Corti

Broca's aphasia a speech disorder caused by damage to Broca's area; marked by poor grammar and short, disconnected sentences

Broca's area the area on the left side of the brain that contains the motor speech area and controls movement of the tongue, lips, and vocal cords

cerebral hemispheres the left and right sides of the brain, connected by a bundle of nerve fibers called the corpus callosum; the left hemisphere contains areas specializing in the production and comprehension of language and is associated with orderly thinking; the right hemisphere contains areas specializing in visual perception, music, and emotions and is associated with nonverbal responses

cerumen ear wax; secreted by the auditory canal to filter out potentially damaging dust and flying insects

coarticulation the phenomenon in which individual sounds in speech overlap and mix

cochlea the snail-shaped, liquid-filled cavity of the inner ear that contains the basilar membrane and the organ of Corti

complex tones tones produced by periodic sounds with a complicated pattern of sound waves; more common than pure tones

conduction aphasia acquired language problem in which the speaker uses inappropriate sounds or words despite good language comprehension

conductive hearing impairment hearing disorder that occurs when sound waves cannot travel properly through the outer or middle ear

cricoid cartilage cartilage that makes up the base of the larynx

critical period period ending at puberty after which children find it difficult, if not impossible, to learn language

decibel unit for measuring sound level or magnitude of sound

developmental language problems problems that occur when a person fails to acquire a complete set of language skills; can be aided by speech-language therapy

disfluency the problem in which speech is not fluid or fluent; commonly experienced by children between two and a half and three and a half years of age when they are trying to graduate from one- and two-word utterances to more complex sentences; a long-lasting problem for some adults

displaced speech speech about things removed in time or space; a feature of speech shared only by humans and a few animals

Doppler effect the phenomenon that produces a higher frequency and pitch from objects moving rapidly closer and a lower frequency and pitch from objects moving rapidly away; caused by the crowding of sound waves with less distance to travel from an object drawing near and by the stretching of sound waves with greater distance to travel from an object moving away

duality of patterning the ability of humans to combine a small pool of sounds to form a vast stock of words

eustachian tube an air-filled canal running from the middle ear to the back of the throat; assures that air pressure in the middle ear remains the same as the pressure outside the ear

frequency feature of a periodic wave; the number of sound waves that pass a specific point within one second

fundamental frequency the lowest frequency component of a complex tone; the pure tone of which all other frequencies in a complex tone are multiples

gestural theory the theory putting forth that those early humans possessing a particularly well developed left hemisphere of the brain (which not only controls the right hand but also serves as the brain's speech center) had nimble right hands, better toolmaking abilities, and consequently an increased chance of survival; suggests that speech ability and the brain developed together

harmonics the components of a complex tone that are multiples of the fundamental frequency

hesitation pause pause in speech that is made within a clause; accounts for 95% of silence during speech; placement suggests an overlap in the planning and production of clauses

hyoid bone the horseshoe-shaped bone that holds the larynx in place; only bone in the human vocal tract

inner ear the part of the ear that contains the cochlea, basilar membrane, organ of Corti, and the auditory nerve; the part of the ear where sound vibrations are transformed into nerve impulses

intonation the rising and falling of the pitch of a person's voice during a sentence due to increases and decreases in the fundamental frequency; adds meaning and expression to speech

language words used in communication, their pronunciation, and the rules needed to combine them.

larynx voice box; an hourglass-shaped organ formed by four pieces of fibrous flexible tissue; located at the top of the trachea; contains the vocal folds

middle ear the part of the ear that converts sound waves carried from the outer ear into mechanical vibrations using the tympanic membrane (eardrum) and three bones (the malleus, incus, and stapes); sends intensified sound waves to the inner ear by way of the membranous oval window

morphology the formation of words through the addition of prefixes and suffixes and by the use of inflection

motor theory the speech reception theory put forth by Alvin Liberman that suggests that people understand what others say by referring to the way that they themselves produce speech

myoelastic-aerodynamic theory of phonation the theory that describes how muscle (myo) tension and flexibility (elastic) combine with air movement (aerodynamics) to create audible puffs of air; disproved the theory that the larynx produces sound by muscular vibration

natural resonant frequency the frequency at which an object will vibrate once set in motion

operant conditioning a form of education using trial, error, and reward; believed by psychologist B. F. Skinner to be the method through which humans acquire language

organ of Corti the organ that rests on the basilar membrane inside the cochlear partition; contains two sets of hair cells that respond to vibrations of the basilar membrane and transform them into nerve impulses

otitis media inflammation of the middle ear; a common conductive hearing impairment

otosclerosis conductive hearing impairment caused by a hardening of the middle ear bones

palate the roof of the mouth, separating the mouth from the nasal cavity; part of the vocal tract; acts as both an acoustic resonator and a surface on which the tongue presses to produce certain consonants

passive theory of speech perception the theory putting forth that speech perception is a sensory activity in which the listener recognizes constant features of speech and uses them to interpret what is being said

period the amount of time needed for a sound wavelength to pass a single point in space

periodic sound the sound produced by an object that vibrates in a repetitive pattern; produces tones

pharynx the muscular tube containing the larynx

phase the state of sound wave in regard to its being either in a state of compression (molecules at a high pressure) or rarefaction (molecules at a low pressure) at a particular point in time and space

phoneme the smallest unit of sound that differentiates one word from another; the smallest divisible unit of language

phonology the system of sounds used in language

pinna auricle; portion of the ear that is visible from the outside; funnels sounds into the auditory canal while amplifying higher frequencies

pitch the subjective perception of sound frequency that can be described as higher and lower notes on a musical scale

pragmatics the use of language in social situations

presbycusis hearing impairment resulting from degenerative changes associated with old age

productivity the human ability to use existing words to create an essentially infinite variety of sentences to express thoughts and ideas

prosody the rhythm and tonal patterns of speech

selection errors speech errors that occur when a person chooses the wrong word for a particular sentence

semantics the study of the meanings of words and signs

sensorineural hearing impairment hearing loss caused by damage to the inner ear, usually in the hair cells of the organ of Corti; tends to affect some frequencies more than others

sound spectrogram the device invented by Ralph Potter that analyzes and graphs the changing frequencies of speech

sound wave an alternating sequence of compression and rarefaction produced by a vibrating object

spreading activation the method used to retrieve words from memory; triggers phonetic and semantic associations until the correct word is found

superior speech cortex a small area near the top of the brain that plays a minor role in the motor functions of speech

syntax the structure or arrangement of words in a phrase, clause, or sentence

telegraphic speech multiword sentences lacking plurals, prepositions, and other refinements of grammar; type of speech used by children as their language abilities develop past one- and two-word phrases

thyroid cartilage a V-shaped cartilage shield that forms the front wall of the larynx and to which the vocal folds attach; in men, creates the bulge in the neck called the Adam's apple

traditional transmission cultural transmission; the learning of human language as passed from generation to generation; distinguishes humans from other animals, whose communication appears to be mainly inherited

tympanic membrane eardrum; a thin membrane at the end of the auditory canal that vibrates in response to sound waves and in turn vibrates the three bones of the inner ear

vocal folds the ligaments and muscles located in the narrow portion of the larynx that produce the sound waves of the human voice by opening and closing rapidly over air pushed by the lungs

vocalis muscles the vibrating part of the vocal folds; the two muscles that stretch between the thyroid and arytenoid cartilages

vocal ligaments the bands of elastic tissue that stretch between the thyroid and arytenoid cartilages; part of the vocal folds

vocal system the lungs, larynx, and vocal tract

vocal tract the nasal cavity, oral cavity, and pharynx; acts as a resonator that amplifies some sound wave frequencies produced in the larynx and muffles others in addition to producing its own sounds; a lowered larynx, a flexible tongue, and evenly spaced teeth enable humans to produce a wider range of sounds than can their closest relative, the ape

Voder Voice Operation Demonstrator; an electronic speech synthesizer invented by Homer Dudley in the 1930s; designed to copy the acoustic features of speech rather than the physical features and motions

voice disorders problems with the pitch, loudness, or quality of a person's speech resulting from improperly vibrating vocal folds (which can be caused, for example, by abnormal growths on the folds) or from a physical deformity such as a cleft palate

wavelength the physical distance between repeating points on a sound wave

Wernicke's aphasia the communication disorder in which the patient speaks in fluent, complete sentences that have little or no meaning; caused by damage to Wernicke's area

Wernicke's area an area located in the left side of the brain behind the left ear that plays an important role in the comprehension of language

INDEX

PICTURE CREDITS

William D. Allstetter is a free-lance science writer based in New York City. He previously worked for 5 years as a newspaper reporter in California and New Mexico and has received both state and national journalism awards. His articles have appeared in *Discover* and *Omni* magazines. Allstetter has a B.A. in human biology from Stanford University and an M.A. from the Columbia University Graduate School of Journalism.

Dale C. Garell, M.D., is medical director of California Children Services, Department of Health Services, County of Los Angeles. He is also associate dean for curriculum at the University of Southern California School of Medicine and clinical professor in the Department of Pediatrics & Family Medicine at the University of Southern California School of Medicine. From 1963 to 1974, he was medical director of the Division of Adolescent Medicine at Children's Hospital in Los Angeles. Dr. Garell has served as president of the Society for Adolescent Medicine, chairman of the youth committee of the American Academy of Pediatrics, and as a forum member of the White House Conference on Children (1970) and White House Conference on Youth (1971). He has also been a member of the editorial board of the *American Journal of Diseases of Children*.

C. Everett Koop, M.D., Sc.D., is former Surgeon General, deputy assistant secretary for health, and director of the Office of International Health of the U.S. Public Health Service. A pediatric surgeon with an international reputation, he was previously surgeon-in-chief of Children's Hospital of Philadelphia and professor of pediatric surgery and pediatrics at the University of Pennsylvania. Dr. Koop is the author of more than 175 articles and books on the practice of medicine. He has served as surgery editor of the *Journal of Clinical Pediatrics* and editor-in-chief of the *Journal of Pediatric Surgery*. Dr. Koop has received nine honorary degrees and numerous other awards, including the Denis Brown Gold Medal of the British Association of Paediatric Surgeons, the William E. Ladd Gold Medal of the American Academy of Pediatrics, and the Copernicus Medal of the Surgical Society of Poland. He is a chevalier of the French Legion of Honor and a member of the Royal College of Surgeons, London.